8
5/1

Joan Dale

D1108268

OF MEN AND WOMEN

BY PEARL S. BUCK

Of Men and Women

PEARL S. BUCK

THE JOHN DAY COMPANY

NEW YORK

Copyright © 1971 by Pearl S. Buck
Copyright 1941 (renewed) by Pearl S. Buck
All rights reserved. No part of this book may be reprinted, or reproduced or
utilized in any form or by any electronic, mechanical or other means, now
known or hereafter invented, including photo-copying and recording, or in
any information storage and retrieval system, without permission in writing
from the Publisher.

The John Day Company, 257 Park Avenue South, New York, N.Y. 10010
An Intext Publisher

Published on the same day in Canada by Longman Canada Limited.

Library of Congress Catalogue Card Number: 75-159970
Printed in the United States of America

FOREWORD

A NOVELIST needs, perhaps, to give no reasons for writing a book about men and women. Men and women are not only his materials but his life, and in their lives the novelist lives in a fashion which can scarcely be explained and which must be accepted. Why such material should be presented in this book, however, may be explained.

When I came to my own country after living most of my life in China, where the pattern for men and women was fixed, I found two obvious things which others coming here from abroad have mentioned more than once: the general discontent of our women and the marked lack of enjoyment between men and women. It takes no very keen observation to see these facts, though doubtless they are clearer to a newcomer than to those who live here. But I am less interested in the facts than in the reasons for them. Why, in a country such as ours, where woman is given every privilege and as much opportunity apparently as she wants, should she be so often dissatisfied in herself and so restless an influence in society? And why should man not like her better than he does?

In trying to find the answers to these questions I naturally reconsidered the old Chinese scheme of family life which is in such contrast to our own. Whether that scheme provides more possibility for happiness than ours and what sort of men and women developed under it as compared to ours made interesting speculation. My conclusion will be clear enough. It is simply that complete freedom is the atmosphere in which men and women can live together most happily. But it must be complete.

One final question may be asked. Why should this book be published now? Because time presses. In a strange and ominous way the fate of women everywhere in the world is linked with the trend toward fascism. To delay might mean to be compelled to silence.

P. S. B.

CONTENTS

1 . THE DISCORD

IT HAS been my good fortune always to have found near me women of good sense. My earliest recollections center about two such women each in her way typical of her society. They were my American mother and my Chinese nurse. Although these two women were different in every moment of their history, they were curiously alike. My mother was the most capable and interesting woman I have ever known. Unusually well educated for her period, she was cultivated, humorous, brilliant, and strong. Though she went to China when she was twenty-three and died there forty-one years later, she remained unchanged by any Chinese influence. She developed from within, as American as if she had remained in her native land.

My nurse, Wang Amah, was almost as forceful, capable, and strong as my mother. She was illiterate but civilized, the daughter of a merchant family in the rich city of Yangchow. In some dire incident of her life my mother had rescued her, and the two women remained together from the moment they met until my nurse died a very old woman. In front of others they were mistress and servant, but when they were alone, especially in the evening before dinner when Wang Amah brushed for an hour my

11

mother's long dark hair, their talk was intimately human
and they were friends. My mother, it is true, confided to
no one her own personal difficulties, but she had the
genius of comforting wisdom which drew from others all
their story. People came for miles over hilly roads and cob-
blestones only to tell her their sorrows. They were mostly
women. I was a solitary child, quiet and often unnoticed,
and talk went on before me. Very early, therefore, I per-
ceived that women together led a life of their own.

For the life of Chinese women in those days, only recently past, fell into an inviolable pattern. Their place
was in the home. The phrase is familiar the world over.
But the Chinese woman, accepting it, made out of home
something that I have seen nowhere else. In China the
home was not what it is in our country, a thing apart from
men's lives except when they return to it for food and
sleep. The real life of the nation went on in the home. Even
men were made an integral part of the home which Chinese women ruled, for the whole fabric of society was
woven there in the intense and complicated life of great
households where three or four generations lived under
connecting roofs. Woman in China had little cause, one
would have said, for ambition outside the home, for all
her managerial ability was needed to oversee the vast
organization of old and young for which she was responsible. Religion, embodied in ancestor worship and temple
visiting and the proper celebration of festivals and the
rites necessary at birth and marriage and death, government, in the administering of the rules of civil law which

gave even the criminal over to clan judgment, education, of boys for professions and business and of girls in training for their marriage, the comforting of the old, the care of the sick, responsibility for poor relatives—all these were the duties of women within the home.

It is no wonder, then, that the Chinese woman generally developed into a strong, wise, able human being, whether she could read or not. Literacy mattered peculiarly little to her. Women handed down to women a vast lore of history, custom, ritual, and practical knowledge which educated them and made them a part of the great national whole. But more valuable than any actual knowledge was the quiet and conscious conviction Chinese women have always had of their own worth. Look at a Chinese woman anywhere in the world, and you will see a human being of personality and poise who apologizes for nothing that she is or does, and in whose calm eyes shines her clear and tranquil soul. She knows her irreducible value as a woman. She does not worry about herself as compared to man. She accepts her difference and knows herself equal to him.

Indeed, she made so honorable her qualities, the so-called feminine qualities, that they began to be accepted as the essentials of a civilized people. Thus the he-man in China came to be considered not as male but merely as uncivilized. "The qualities of the feminine intelligence," says Lin Yutang in *My Country and My People,* "are exactly the qualities of the Chinese mind." Thus did the power

13

of woman grow in China as she gathered the nation's life into its homes and ruled there.

I took woman's equality with man for granted, therefore, until I came to live in my own country seven years ago. American women I had known abroad, though in no great numbers. Those few were, I have found since, on the whole unusual women. I suppose there must always be something unusual in a woman who is willing to cross oceans and make a home on alien earth. Those American women did not differ too much from Chinese women except in outward habits. But I learned from them, and indeed my mother had already told me, that these habits signified something. The freedom with which American women went out of their homes, the informality with which they talked to men, and the whole spontaneity of their behavior were all signs of a free society. The pattern of men and women, I then learned for the first time, was different in America from the fixed and static pattern of men and women in China.

When I returned to my own country to live, therefore, I expected to find men and women really equal—that is, that the affairs of the nation, large and small, were carried on by both alike. By this time there had been a revolution in China which had opened the doors of home and let women out. They came out poised, assured, self-confident, accustomed to executive responsibility; and they swarmed into schools, industries, and business, and even into government offices. I expected, of course, to see women in

America even more assured and competent. Were they not long accustomed to participation in all parts of life?

My first surprise came when I asked for the name of a good bank, preferably a bank managed by women. Friends of mine had used a women's bank in Shanghai and had liked the way women there had handled investments. They found women astute, daring and cautious together. But in my own country, I was told, there is no bank owned and managed by women. When I asked why, I was told that no one would put money in such a bank. I have not to this day found the reason for this.

The next surprise came when I searched for a woman doctor, since I share the preference of Chinese women for women physicians to attend them. But I was told, and by women, that there are very few first-rate doctors in our country who are women. Most women here, it seems, even prefer men about them when they are in childbirth, although to my thinking then of all times the physician should be a woman. How can any man, however learned and sensitive, really understand the situation of a woman bearing a child? It is the one experience he cannot fully comprehend. Again, I have not yet been able to discover a reason for this preference for the male, though I persevered and found for myself an excellent physician who is also a woman.

Surprise followed upon surprise. Where I had expected in a free society to find women working everywhere as men worked, according to their ability, I found them actually less influential by far than women had been under the traditional scheme of life in China.

It is more than that woman's influence is almost totally lacking in the centers of American national life. She has somehow so conducted herself besides that her feminine qualities, which are her greatest gift and power, have come to be despised and looked upon as effeminate. Far from permeating society so that a civilized people came to despise crude force and to trust to reason, women in our country have even upheld the crudity of force as a desirable male attribute and have continued blind to the fact that in so doing they have fostered a society in which crude force manifests itself in gangsters and in wars. Somewhere in the home before even they go to school little boys learn to think that the superior male is tough and rough, and they struggle to form themselves on the model. I have actually heard American mothers tell their sons, "Don't be a sissy girl. You are a boy." If a certain kind of male is desired, I can understand this education, but what is one to think of women who deliberately teach their sons to despise women? Is it necessary to make the female inferior in order that the male may feel himself, or even be, superior? Then what unjust inferiority is this, and how frail a superiority! It is no wonder that woman is of no real consequence in the life of our nation.

And yet as I write these words I question them. I sit here this morning in the old American farmhouse which is my home and think of many women of good sense in my immediate neighborhood. They are in almost every house working with quiet energy and intelligence to create order and comfort for their families. They are part of a community which I know is not unique, whose women as a matter of course work in homes and factories and upon farms. They carry on a tradition for women which I like to think of as peculiarly American, a classless tradition which makes it possible for a woman to scrub and clean a house, cook a fine meal, husk corn for twenty to thirty cents an hour in this region or do piece work in a shirt or pants factory or a hosiery mill and earn from ten to twenty-five dollars a week, and on occasion and certainly here on Sunday put on a good silk dress and look what she is, a "lady." She is, I say, a lady all the time. Her good sense makes her equal to any occasion. I watched one of her kind yesterday at work in her kitchen, thinking as I watched, "There—she's what I mean by an American woman."

Actually she was born in Hungary and came to America as one of a large family of children. Her parents farmed, and she grew up on American bread and milk and meat and fruit and garden stuff to be tall and strong and handsome, as she still is. She married young, a farmer, and they had six children. She kept house and cared for the children, and in the afternoon worked in the fields. To this day, though she is well over fifty, she loves to go out into the field. When she cries out, "Ah, I got to git my hands in the dirt," I know it is spring.

Her husband died early, and she was left a young widow with six children. What shall I tell of those years except that she managed, keeping her house and her children by washing and cooking for others or by any work she could find? The children are all grown up now, independent except for the youngest girl, and the first boy was married last year. She said the other day, her eyes misting, "I'm to be a grandmother by next Christmas." I knew by the satisfaction in her voice that the circle of her life was completed for her.

And she is not alone. There are many like her. I condoled with a neighbor's son the other day over the loss of a job. He said, " 'Taint' too bad, for my wife works in the factory and she can hold us together till I get somethin'."

"Do most women work outside the home around here," I asked, "or do you have an unusual wife?"

"No, she ain't unusual—not like that, I mean," he said. "Women mostly help out their menfolks around here."

"Do you think," I persisted, "that they help out more than they used to?"

"No," he said. "Can't say as it's any different now from what it ever was. My wife's mother worked in the shirt factory—still does; and my own mother worked in the hosiery. Reckon we're all used to work around here."

Roughly speaking, almost half of the women of America are used to work in this sense. They are busy, steady-hearted women, contributing their full share to their homes or to the community industry or to both. They are women of great good sense. Seeing their quiet competence and plain wisdom, I often wish that it could find wider use. This competence, this wisdom of life, are what the world lacks in the engine rooms of the nations. But women seem never to be found there, though indeed everywhere else. But why in a country free to them have our women at least not naturally and as a matter of course taken their place with men in the engine rooms of our society? And what of all those other women who need not work full time at home and who do not "help out" their men in field and factory? What are they making of their freedom? They, too, are not in the engine rooms. They are not "helping out" their men at all. Indeed, they live a life singularly separate from the lives of men and the nation's work.

I hold no brief for the old Chinese pattern of men and women. Ours is better, and even if it were not, it is ours and so better for us. And yet I am constrained to ask further, why do so many American women seem not happy in being women when they have the freedom to make what they will of themselves? And why do women and men not enjoy each other more in my country? I was used, in that rich family life of old China, which had its other evils, to this good—the great mutual enjoyment between men and women of all the details and events of the life that they made together. Then which is the best life for men and women, that in a patterned society such as old China had and in another sense as modern Germany has today, or the complete freedom which a true democracy alone can give? I say again, one or the other of the two must be best, for the half-and-half sort of thing we now have patently gives satisfaction to neither man nor woman; and when men and women are not content with and in each other then all of life is discord.

The basic discovery about any people, therefore, is the discovery of the relationship between its men and women. The traveler may tour until a landscape becomes as familiar to him as his own face in a mirror, but if he has not from experience or intimate observation in a country comprehended the way men and women feel toward each other, the measure of their understanding of each other, and the place each has in the life of the whole, the reality of that country has escaped him.

The fundamentals of men and women are the same anywhere. This difference in human beings, created into men and women, is common to us all. It is a difference more universal, deeper, more important than the differences of race and nation, and yet it is the one most ignored. One generalization only can be made on the ways in which men and women live together. When there is harmony between men and women the culture of a country—that is, its whole life—is full, peaceful, and without nervous tensions, and progress is steady and rounded. Men and women enjoy each other then to the extent that their social customs allow, and this enjoyment is a fair indication of harmony between them. But when the relationship between men and women is confused and there is no harmony, and when they cannot much enjoy each other, then the general life is full of tension and irritations and strains. Point me out a people emotional, restless, argumentative, impulsive, volatile, changeable, violent in its prejudices, and

I will point you out a people where men and women are at odds with each other, whether they know it or not or will admit it or not. Fortitude in hardships, good sense and balance in prosperity, a sense of proportion at all times—these are the fruits of harmony between men and women in a nation.

And effects seemingly quite remote may nevertheless be direct results of the fundamental lack of harmony. A widespread feeling of insecurity, for instance, commonly attributed to economic causes, is, I believe, far more to be ascribed to the deep emotional insecurity of men and women in each other. When they are uncertain of each other, doubtful of each other's loyalty either as individuals or as groups, there arises in every heart a feeling of isolation and solitariness that is hateful to it. For no human being was created to be solitary, and when it is cut off by doubt and distrust and lack of understanding from the other to whom instinctively it turns, whom nature has created for it, then strange stops and blocks and ills are inescapable. When in a period of social change the whole relationship of men and women shifts for a time as established customs break down and new ones have not yet been made, then necessarily, too, this cosmic loneliness besets the individual and undermines all his being and adds to the confusion of the times—which, indeed, to some extent it may have caused. So when men and women are not in harmony, when their lives and works are separate or contradictory, then all of life seems unsafe and dangerous. The prevailing national mood becomes despondent and fearful, and even figures and facts of increasing prosperity do not lighten it. Men and women can face anything, can endure anything, if they are sure of each other's loyalty and liking. They can endure nothing if they are not sure of each other.

Nor can individuals hope to escape the effects of the larger despondency about them. There will always be plenty of romantically happy marriages begun in each generation. Whether a fair number of these will continue to be happy will depend not only upon the couples but far more than they realize upon the relationship of men and women as a whole in their time. Discontent between those who can be fully happy only when there is content between them will arise too often even between two who are individually content with each other. For man remains man to the end of his days, and woman remains woman; and too often it is true that these two never meet. It is a tragedy when they do not, because there is no joy like the joy of life when they do.

And I do not mean only the meeting of marriage. For marriage is only one of the ways of meeting between the two kinds of human beings. Every part of life has the possibility of the joy of their full meeting. All of life is right for men only if women they value comprehend and approve them for what they are, and all of life is right for women only if men they value comprehend and approve them. Love may have something to do with this once or twice in a lifetime, but most of the time it does not, and to assume that it does is to limit at once the whole relationship between men and women to what is only one of its expressions.

Of course men and women have some sort of relationship to each other from the moment they are born baby boys and girls to the moment that they die old men and women. They are never freed of each other, however great their love or dislike. For dislike is a relationship as valid as love, and true indifference is probably impossible. When indifference is proclaimed its very proclamation denies its reality. There is no use in pretending that men and women are not supremely important to each other, for they are, everywhere. A wise people recognizes this and provides for it in rational ways, and calmness in the national temper is the result.

When the ancient Chinese deliberately chose and developed to its highest point the traditional pattern of life which kept woman within the walls of home they did all they could to help her. They bound the feet of women so that they could not hobble many yards from their own gates, but they bound their minds also with fetters of ignorance and decreed that women were not to be given the general learning that was given to men. Women as a rule were not allowed even the opportunity to read and write. The Chinese were wise and humane in this. Having decided definitely that the place of woman was in the home and that in the home she was to stay, they arranged to confine her mind there as well as her body so that she did not know for centuries that she was a prisoner. What exquisite horrible torture had they bound her feet alone and then

liberated her mind! What agony to sit behind a wall beyond which she could not go and contemplate a world alive
with activity and enjoyment and discovery but forbidden
to her!

But no, the Chinese, merciful to their women, spared
them such torture. Women lived in their homes quietly
and happily ignorant and embroidered pretty little shoes
for their crippled feet, little shoes they never took off even
at night lest men see the real deformity they hid. They
made of their feet "golden lilies," and men fondled them
as acts of love and wrote poems about them. The tiny
feet of Chinese women were for centuries sexual symbols.
Men felt their passions stir merely at the sight of a
woman's embroidered pointed satin shoe, three inches
long and the width of two fingers. And when modern
times came, it was women who did not want to give up
their little feet. They had for so long wielded their power
over men by those little feet.

Women had grown very powerful. Within the confines
of their lives, narrow in space, they had gone deep and
climbed high. They had come to understand completely
the nature of men. They knew men's every weakness and
used such weakness ruthlessly for their own ends, good or
evil. Lacking other education, they devised cunning and
wile and deviousness and charm, and they had men wholly
in their power, confounding simple men by their wisdom
and learned men by their childishness. Men had to feed,
clothe, and shelter them. Men had to work for them, fight
for them, and protect them. Man's one reward they gave

him. It was to allow him a feeling of superiority because he was a male, and as they granted him this in seeming generosity, they hid their smiles behind their pretty embroidered sleeves.

The greatest evil in this old Chinese scheme of life for men and women was that it was so unfair to men. As women in the home grew too powerful men were weakened and warped by them, and became helpless. For woman, confined to her home by long custom until she looked on it as her natural sphere and had no desire to go beyond it, became a tyrant there. If she were stupid she ruined man's digestion by being too good a cook and by insisting that he eat all she cooked. Or she encouraged him to take his ease and not to exert himself and even though he gladly yielded he had his hours of uncomfortable remorse because he knew he was wasting his life. And yet the stupid woman in the house was not worse than the intelligent woman there, who by her restless energy drove man to do what he did not want to do and more than he wanted to do, compelling him to fulfill her rather than himself.

The misfortune is, of course, that women are quite often born with brains. The scheme which limits woman to homes should provide some means against her inheriting an intelligence equal to man's, which she does not need. If all women could be born with inferior minds and men with superior ones, the scheme of women for the home would doubtless be perfectly satisfactory. But unless that can be done, it is not satisfactory. Four thousand years of Chinese experience prove it. The eminently rational Chinese did everything they could to ensure harmony between men and women in the pattern of tradition. They kept woman ignorant and limited her to the home and its cares and to the breeding of children. They made having children woman's chief duty and greatest glory. They heaped honor upon the mothers of sons. Moreover, they actually accomplished what has been so far an impossible achievement in the western countries such as the United States and England: the Chinese gave marriage to every woman. This, they thought, was only fair. They said, if society decrees that woman's place is in the home, then it is but justice to see that every woman has a home to go to; anything else is unrealistic.

But such justice they knew had to be made compulsory. It cannot be left to men alone. For, as the Chinese found a good many centuries before we did, too many men, left to themselves, will not marry. To marry, man discovered long ago, is a very serious matter for him. For one thing, it fixes the responsibility of fatherhood. If a man is not married to a woman, there is always the chance that he is not a father. But when he is the only man to whom the woman is accessible, there is no escape for him. He has to support his offspring and the woman, too. And a surprisingly small number of men are natural fathers, the ancient Chinese found. Far too many have fatherhood thrust upon them. It was in fact a disagreeable awakening for men in early Chinese history when they discovered indisputably that there was a definite relation between sleeping with a woman and an infant some months later. Women suspected the connection long before men did and then be-came convinced of it. But men only reluctantly came to believe it.

When it was formally acknowledged to be true, how-ever, the Chinese in their rational way organized their life around the fact. Since children came of men and women together, they must live together for the children. But man had no idea of giving up his private freedom to this agreement. He would feed the woman and child and provide their shelter. In that shelter they must stay, but he would continue to roam as he pleased. This was the beginning of home for the woman. And so woman stayed in it, century after century, and she was kept ignorant ex-cept of cooking and sewing and elementary child care, while man continued to roam—that is, he was educated for the activities of business, government, and the arts, and all the life outside the home.

Thus marriage was made obligatory. This was not, of course, so stated. The Chinese are a subtle people. They do not make laws and expect people automatically to obey them. Neither do they believe in the efficacy of force upon human beings except as a necessity for some temporary occasion. They know that if people can be persuaded to want to do a thing, it is the most permanent way of achiev-ing that end. In order to make marriage obligatory, there-fore, the Chinese encouraged ancestor worship. They knew that the human individual fears above all else the extinction of death, and they proclaimed the doctrine that if a man had sons he did not die. The worship his sons gave his spirit when his body died kept him alive, they said. Therefore a man ought to have sons, the more the better, since so many children inevitably died young. But that he might have legal sons, and sons he was sure were from his own seed, he must marry. The price of a man's immortality was thus made to depend on marriage, and only when this came about did men take marriage as a necessity. Then fathers arranged for the marriage of their sons and women were encouraged to make breeding their chief duty so that when a woman was barren, if she were a truly good woman, she did not complain if her husband brought other women into the house. She even encouraged him to do so, denying her own heart that Right might be done.

It was called Right, of course, or people would not have denied themselves to do it. The wise Chinese knew that nothing so nerves and strengthens the poor average human heart as a demand put upon it for noble self-sacrifice in the cause of some Right. So throughout the centuries many an ignorant Chinese woman with all her pitiful heart has bade her beloved take another in her place to give him the sons she could not give him. It is not easy—it was never easy. I have heard their sad stories of how the night through they have stuffed their quilts into their mouths, silk quilts, ragged quilts, so that men could not hear the sound of weeping. But they always believed their men were doing right.

There was another wisdom in this custom, too. By some strange will of Nature, women are everywhere stronger

in body than men are, and they can live when men must
die; and so there are nearly always too many women. This
grew dangerous in China, for the natural resistance of the
female there was fortified by the handicaps of her existence. She was spared the coddling and dainty feeding and
all that whole weakening process of spoiling that was given
to the precious boys; and so girls lived, unfortunately,
when boys died. Polygamy was the only resource if woman
was to be kept in the home. Except the deliberate infanti-
cides of girls, polygamy will be the only resource in any
country that insists that women be kept in the home, and
especially if warfare is to be the chief occupation of the
men. In spite of the fact that modern warfare today kills
more women and children than it once did, the death rate
for men is still likely to be higher than it is for women.
So polygamy was made legal in old China.

All might still have worked out well enough for men
and women in that clearly defined Chinese scheme of life
if unfortunately women had not continued to be born
with brains which no limitation, physical or mental, could
subdue. There were too many clever women, too many intelligent women, everywhere in every household. These
restless creatures, finding themselves ignorant and kept
within walls, did not, as they should have done, subside
into quiescence or content. Instead they occupied themselves with getting their own way and with becoming
powerful in any fashion they could.

"You do not know," Reynaud sighed in fallen France

only the other day, "to what lengths a man will go to secure an evening's peace!"

So has sighed many a man in China, returning to his home at night to face a strong, willful, intelligent woman whose whole too-able mind concentrates itself upon him. If she is beautiful, and she is more often beautiful than not, for she knows beauty is one of his weaknesses, he is lost before he ever opens the door to her chamber, and helplessly he knows it.

Long before modern China gave to women complete equality woman in China was man's superior. In fact, I have even suspected that when the modern revolution came he was glad to insist on her becoming only equal with him at last. It was a forward step for him, and she lost by it. She had to stop being a willful creature who made the most of her ignorance and who got all she wanted by pretending to be childish and irresponsible and weak and charming while actually she was strong, tough, executively able and mentally shrewd. It was man in China who hastened to write into the constitution that woman had to be equal with him and accept equal responsibility as an adult individual. He gladly threw open all schools and professions to her, and what must his satisfaction be today as he sees her take up her gun and march beside him to battle!

Yes, for any nation contemplating the return of woman to the home, I recommend before taking the step a thorough study of the history of Chinese men and women, for there women had the best of it. They used their ignorance to confound men's wisdom. As ignorant creatures, they had no necessity for rational behavior, and they early saw this. Tempers and tantrums, and fads and whimsies—what else, men said, could they expect from women? When they came home tired at night they yielded anything for peace.

And being ignorant, women, though powerful, were not even good mothers to men. Too many of their sons died young and teaching them elementary child care did little good. For the uneducated mind cannot really be taught anything. It grows up preoccupied with its own ignorant ideas. It is convinced of its own rightness. Only the truly educated mind knows the possibility of error. And so the ignorant Chinese mother was always sure, secretly, that there was nothing in any new idea; and if she was stupid besides, then she was unteachable, and her beloved sons suffered from the very excess of her love.

Thus do men always suffer when women are ignorant. They suffer more than women, not only because women are stronger than men and more resistant, but because men are peculiarly vulnerable to the damage ignorant women can do at the periods of their life when they most need intelligent and wise care: in infancy, in adolescence, in times of illness and mental and emotional crisis, and in old age. Wise Chinese saw this, too, and endeavored to mitigate the danger by taking boys out of the care of women early in childhood. Thus boys as young as seven were taken into the quarters for men. But fathers were often away from home and mothers were always there, and boys ran back to women who indulged and spoiled them and fed them with sweets—all with loving intention.

Through loving intention century after century Chinese men grew weak at the hands of women.

For men cannot be free in a nation where women are forbidden freedom. China has found that out at last. To-day every door stands open to men and women alike. This was true even before the war, but war has hastened the equalizing process. What will happen when war is over and the complex problems of peace begin once more? Who knows? But I do not believe that those gates will close again. If there is even any danger of it, the problems of peace being always more difficult than those of war, I believe that Chinese men and women will pause and look at each other and remember what life was like between them for four thousand years. "Anything but that," they will say, and they will go on together to face the future that none today can see.

2. THE HOME IN CHINA
AND AMERICA

T HE American home I know very well, partly from close observation of homes during the years that I have been living in my own country, but as much from my own typically American home in China. My parents were Americans, patriotic to their core, and simply and honestly convinced, as most Americans are, that the American home is the best in the world. To them American home life was even a part of the Christian religion which they felt it their duty and privilege to preach to the Chinese. I do not believe it ever occurred to my parents in the goodness of their saintly hearts to ask themselves whether or not the Chinese had a sort of home life which was perhaps as valuable in its way as ours, or at least better suited to China than ours was.

Our home, therefore, was kept absolutely and carefully American. We had American furniture and American food, though all of us children liked Chinese food better, and only as a concession to our pleading did we have an occasional Chinese meal. Beyond that we satisfied our cravings by partaking heartily of the servants' meals before our own and listening in guilty silence to our mother worrying over our small appetites. We got up in the morning and had prayers and ate porridge and eggs for breakfast and studied our American lessons, and on Sundays a Christian church bell rang and we went to church, and the only difference was that the Christians in that church were Chinese instead of American. We were trained in all the ways of American homemaking, and spiritually we were kept close not to the Chinese about us but to our own loved land thousands of miles away that we had never known except through our parents' eyes and words.

So perfectly did they succeed in their determination to make us good Americans that, after half a lifetime spent away from my own country, I came back to it without any feeling of being alien or strange. All seemed my own, and I was native to it. For this I must thank my American home in China, for after my childhood I myself deliberately departed from American ways and plunged myself deep into China. I went into parts of China to live where few white people were ever seen and spent much of my time in Chinese homes where a white woman had never been before; and there, in long quiet talk with women whose lives had been shaped on a pattern totally different from mine, I learned again the inwardness of Chinese homes, as a woman now and not as I had when I was a child playing with Chinese children. One experience was as valuable as the other, and each throws light upon the other. I cannot say which I consider the better, the Chinese or the American home.

I mention the Chinese home, therefore, not to compare

it favorably to the American home but to define the American home more sharply by contrast. As I think of that contrast, I see it first at the point of contact between the home and the world outside. A child in China finds the world inside his home. The world is indeed inside the walls of his house in all its generations. When he enters it he does not even come into a single house and garden. He comes into several or many courtyards and houses, depending upon the economic status of the family. Here in these separate or semiconnected buildings in these courtyards leading from one to the other live all the large family, the grandparents or eldest males and their wives at its head, and their children and grandchildren. Each couple has more or less private quarters for sleep, but the meals are often communal except where men eat first together and then women, and all during the day life goes on in common. Even a poor man's house in China, if it be average, has as a matter of course more than one generation living in it.

Therefore the Chinese child does not think of home as his parents and himself. He is in fact united with his parents in subordinacy to the elders of the composite household. These, with cousins and the inevitable servants, make up a group sufficiently large so that the Chinese child is never or very seldom aware of one single personality dominating the house, as for instance he is inevitably aware in the American home of the personality of the mother. He grows up an individual among individuals, many adults, many children besides himself, with not only the brothers and sisters he almost certainly has in as large a number as his mother can produce them, but all the children of his relatives. He learns to adjust to them, and so when he does leave home he already knows how to get along with people outside. He need not adjust to life because he has adjusted to it from the moment he was born in his own home.

This home, moreover, provides the Chinese child with two other valuable assets: early emotional security and a foundation of economic security. Since the Chinese believe that marriage is a necessity for all and must be provided for everyone exactly as food and shelter are necessary and provided, Chinese parents as their children approach adolescence begin to consider their mating to suitable persons. This is usually not done entirely arbitrarily. The child's temperament is carefully considered, and he is often consulted. In these modern times young people are even shown to each other and given some opportunity for acquaintance. But the expressed object is marriage, and the young people know it. If they like each other they agree to it; if they do not the parents look further. No one talks of love. That is expected to follow marriage, and usually does. This is the ordinary procedure of marriage in China today. It varies from the extreme of parental authority compelling children to marriage to the extreme of free love between certain ultra-moderns.

When with the establishment of the republican form of government in 1911 many national schools were opened for boys and girls and co-education was a matter of course from kindergarten through college, it was inevitable that young people far more frequently than before arranged their own marriages by falling in love. The percentage of unsuccessful marriages among these was much higher than in the arranged marriages. Easy and private divorce was then established to deal with this situation. Chinese have always considered the individual's well-being and happiness of first importance, and tradition changes quickly in that old country when it becomes inconvenient.

Next to emotional security the traditional Chinese home offers economic security of a peculiarly comforting sort. No young man is expected to be able to support a wife at the time he should and does marry. He lives with her in his parents' home and goes on with his education. Pride and family pressure compel him to find work as soon as he can, but family influence helps him even then. Moreover, the home continues its protection all his life. At any time if he loses his job his family helps until he finds another work. In his turn he takes care of his parents as a matter of course when they are old, and himself looks forward to a peaceful old age made secure by his own children's care. There is no talk of the shame of dependence, for he has depended upon his parents and will depend on his children in the cycle of life and there is no shame in it. Thus in China the home and not the state provides the social security for the individual.

When a Chinese child is born, therefore, he is born into the world, not into a nest feathered and shaped to him. It is, moreover, a huge going concern where many persons of all ages are already living busily and he is only one more—precious, loved, if he is a boy often spoiled—but he is always one of a group. By the time he is fifteen he is an adult. If the child is a boy, he has been since he was seven in the special care of men, chief among whom is his father. If the child is a girl, she has been under her mother's special tuition. But each has his place and his work in the vast family institution to which he knows he must in time be a contributing member, but from which, too, he has security as long as he lives. This Chinese home accounts entirely, I believe, for the poise, equanimity, and general emotional stability and gaiety of the Chinese nature. The individual—man, woman, and child—feels himself secure in his place. Whatever the world outside thinks of him, the world of his home is always there, dependent not upon him or his parents alone but upon a group large enough so that if for a time one of them fails as an individual he has those who will help him and share his responsibilities.

It can be truly said, therefore, that in China the home is the bulwark of Chinese national life and the center of Chinese civilization. As the other great democracy at present in the world, this should be of interest to Americans. For these Chinese homes have bred a nation instinctively stubbornly democratic. Chinese society is as fluid and free from hidebound caste as is our own. The log-cabin tradition is centuries old in China, only it is there called the grass-hut tradition. The Chinese admire the self-made man as much as we do, and most of their great men are self-made. But whether the home is a rich man's many courts or a poor man's grass hut, its traditions and customs are fundamentally the same.

Our American home is wholly unlike the Chinese home. The triangle of man, woman, and child is its symbol. Man and woman separate themselves from all others into a solitude of two, and when the child is born he joins this close little world and, in a sense mystic, rapturous, and sometimes tragic, the three become one. The union is either deep and close or it is intolerable, and there is no escape from it except by separation. There is always escape in the Chinese home. If the man and woman are ill-mated, they can escape from each other into the larger family. They can, if they like, see almost nothing of each other. The child, too, can escape his parents easily and without being aware of it. The individual is more easily an individual in that large family. He escapes the hold of deep emotional ties, as well, perhaps, as their satisfaction. Certainly he escapes their almost inevitable overshadowing of his own personality. Nor does he lack affection. The Chinese are a warm race and demonstrative toward their children. Little children are greatly loved and have happy if not always hygienic childhoods. They receive love and approbation from many instead of two. Fortunately for health, the kiss is not a usual Chinese caress, or children would be kissed far too often for their own good.

In the close, small American family, therefore, the primary problem, it seems to me, is the one of maintaining the proper balance between individual life and development and the union necessary to the most successful family life, and in relating the whole to the world beyond. For when the family is small—that is, mother, father, and child—the responsibility upon the parents is greatly increased. The care of the child, physical, emotional, and mental, depends entirely upon those two who have also their own relation to each other to consider and at the same time their own individualities. The many personalities in the large Chinese family undoubtedly have their frictions, but it is debatable at least whether the relations between them are not, from the very number of persons involved, more superficial and therefore less oppressive than the profound tie between a man and a woman who for love choose each other and independently of all others make their life together. There is refuge in the variety of the Chinese family from any one personality; in the primary world of two there is no refuge from each other. Deeper the joy, perhaps, but deeper too the wounds, and more inescapable.

Certainly the small American family does not, in its very structure, train the child so naturally and unconsciously for the world outside. The adjustment from home to outside life is much more severe for the American child than for the Chinese. The American home, indeed, forces the child into a peculiarly contradictory position. It provides a very deep and close emotional life and much and seclusive protection up to a certain age, and then ejects the child into outside life with an abruptness that would horrify the Chinese parent, to whom it would seem unjust to say, for instance, "You must be able to support your wife before you can marry," who would never make a child ashamed at any time, however old he was, of returning to the home for shelter and temporary refuge. Nor on his side does the Chinese child dream of considering his old parents a burden. Their care is his unquestioned duty, as he hopes in his time to be cared for by his son.

Upon consideration of these two types of home, I believe the American home is better and happier when it is ideal than the Chinese home is, but that on a lower scale of idealism the Chinese home meets more adequately the practical needs of the ordinary individual for economic and emotional security.

But China is China, and our country our own, and, while contrast illuminates, it offers no actual solution to our American problems. We are definitely committed to our own way of life. We believe in our tradition of man and woman seeking each other in free mating, and alone and together setting up the home for the child. What can be done to make that pattern as successful as it can be?

It is difficult to answer this question, for the American home is not like the home in any other country. It is still a pioneer home, a relic of days when the adventurous man and woman left the settlement and pushed into the wilderness. The ability to be solitary, independence, resourcefulness, self-sufficiency, were necessary for the pioneer home; and these qualities inevitably developed. And, since the pioneer became a symbol of Americanism, his home became the ideal American home. To go out for oneself, to build for one's own, became American virtues; and fine virtues they are and not to be lost.

But it is necessary to question whether or not the pioneer home fits our no-longer-pioneer times. The last ten years have shown us that, with the best will in the world, even well-trained young men cannot go out and find a place for themselves and their families. We have come to the place that other older nations have reached, of having to adjust our human beings and even their ideals to their times. Thus we have to come to the point of accepting the fact that the generations must help each other more, the elder helping the younger by making properly early marriage possible, and the younger helping to make old age secure. Either the home or the state must do this. China did it through the home and preserved thereby a great deal of individual freedom and independence. We are tending toward state care, and we do not yet know the effects this will have upon the home and the individual. Certainly it seems only reasonable to believe that, human nature being what it is, a person would be less demoralized by family aid than by state aid. He sees the sacrifice of others in the family, but state funds are remote and apparently inexhaustible, and persons soon learn to take such help for granted. Perhaps it should be taken for granted in the future state, but if it is, then the ideals of individual independence must change if character is not to deteriorate.

As I proceed it seems to me that the real problem of the American home today is entirely comprehended in this lack of adjustment between its pioneer form and the no-longer-pioneer times. For of the three, man and child have proceeded with the times, but woman has not, and today the home is too peculiarly hers. Industrial development has taken man out of the home. His workshop is no longer there but in a place not only physically remote but spiritually remote from woman. She used to know, and so to some extent share, what man did when he cleared land, cut down trees, or worked at forge and harness and tavern. But now she not only does not share, she does not even know, what man does. She remains in the pioneer age and is today a creature almost totally alone.

Even her child has been taken from her by the change of time. The child used to be her job, in addition to all her work of keeping the home, preparing food and clothing. She used to teach him how to read and write and always supplemented, as far as she was able, the inadequate pioneer schools. But the schools are no longer pioneer, and the child has moved with the school. He leaves the home at the age of six or earlier, compulsorily, and from then on is returned to woman only for a few of his waking hours.

When women say, therefore, that their place today is in the home, it is a lonely place. The average American woman, especially in the home of average and above-average income, is far too much alone. It is a sharp and devastating loneliness. For woman was once a part of her world, and if it was a world of wilderness, still man and child were with her and together they made a comforting, companionable unit. But now she has not that companionship. She listens to as much as they will tell her, she reads as much as she is inclined, she potters about on the fringe of the world which really goes on without her, and comforts herself by having a good hot dinner ready at night, anyway. It is not enough. The feeling one has after coming to know American women is that they are starving at their sources.

Let me quote from a letter just received from an American woman, a college professor's wife. She says, "To those of us who have thought a good deal about woman's plight it has become a truism that the work which made woman a productive force and gave her a feeling of importance has been taken from home. But the average woman does not realize this: she cannot understand why her housewifely state is not socially satisfying, and, consequently, along with her restlessness goes a destructive sense of guilt."

I believe this woman is right. For the quality of the American woman is high. She is natively intelligent, she has a better education on the average than woman has in any other country. She has, unless she stifles it with tradition, a sensitive conscience. She wants to be of use and to use her powers. But, having been left behind, she does not know what to do. She is not able to make now her home a part of the changing times.

More serious to woman even than the removal of the need for her physical labor is the fact that she is no longer the spiritual and moral influence she was once to man and child in the home. A woman cannot be a source of spiritual power to those two who live apart from her in a vivid, changing world. Their problems are not hers. There is not time to tell her over again all that they have lived in the hours while they have been away from her, and she could not understand or share by mere listening, anyway. If woman is to recapture the lost companionship with man and child she must once more forget herself, as she did in the old pioneer days, and follow them into the world.

I stress woman thus because I believe her peculiar situation is the main root of the problem in the American home today. The burden of a people's transition is being carried mainly by her, and her restlessness and loneliness, whether she is aware of it or not, are irritants in the home and in the nation. In loneliness she puts forth appeals, in one way or another, for companionship from man and child, who are her means of life. They are, according to their natures, either irked or oppressed by these appeals. And yet she has been alone all day. Of course, no one except herself is to blame that she has been alone and lonely. But she does not see that, either. For the American woman has grown into certain mistakes. She has, for instance, grown into the mistake of accepting her separation from men. A young married woman said to me the other day, "We have had to take it for granted that we are married to perpetually tired men. The competition is so fearful these days that it takes all of our men's time just to make a living."

She looked so plump, so healthy, so little tired, that I

45

could not forbear saying, "But why don't you work, too, so that he isn't so tired and so that you can enjoy each other?"

She said, laughing, "Oh, well, it seems as though everything were organized the way it is—it's hard to change things."

If this is the spirit of many American women, then of course they will simply drift into further segregation and into real uselessness and end in some future age in harems and zenanas, and our civilization will be degenerate and ended and democracy dead. For no country is a true democracy whose women have not an equal share in life with men, and until we realize this we shall never achieve a real democracy on this earth. But no country can so much as hope to be a democracy whose women do not even want that share.

I cannot believe that such is the spirit of most American women. The pioneer blood in them cannot be so dead. For the pioneer was willing to leave all he knew and go out and build the world he wanted. Change did not frighten him. There must be women in our country of spirit enough to want to grow with the nation and to stay beside man as he struggles to build. If there are not, then I say that the average woman in the home is the weakest link in American democracy, and by her weakness she drags at the man and hampers the child. By her very love and devotion to them she does this, if that love and devotion are not great enough, not intelligent enough, to comprehend the necessity of sharing their lives with

46

them outside the home as well as the few precious hours within it.

The average American woman ought now, therefore, to be awakened and stimulated and urged—frightened, if need be—into becoming aware of herself and of what she has allowed the world to become because she has not stayed a part of the life of the world as it went out of the home.

And American men, or perhaps I imagine it, would welcome the change in her. It has come to be my conviction, based on observation and conversation and experience, that the more intelligent an American man is, the more troubled he is by the present relationship between man and woman. He would like to have women intelligent and responsible, but he does not know how to get her to want to be. I happened to be sitting at dinner the other night in Washington next to an unusually intelligent congressman. He said, as we talked of this, "The truth is, we give women what they think they want. They want to be babied so we baby them." The depth of contempt in his voice, of which I am sure he was unconscious, made me cringe.

But what he said was true. American women can have what they want. It is not man who keeps woman where she is in our country, but woman herself. Then I was angry. Why should men allow women to become so much less than they could be? Was this not the voice of Adam again, speaking against Eve to accuse her in the matter of the apple? But before I could speak for Eve I remembered how women, too, belittle men. They belittle men when they behave toward man as if he were a protozoa made up of stomach and sex. Read a woman's magazine, a woman's column, and see if there is a reference to be found to any other part of a man's being. And yet there must be more to him, for how otherwise are the affairs of the world managed? It is true that it would be easier for woman if man were all stomach and sex, for then he would stay happily at home with her. That he spends very little of his time with her ought to teach her something about him, but it does not. Instead she only changes her hairdresser and buys new clothes and perfumes and concocts new foods.

Actually the whole business is silly. Men baby women because they think women want it, and women baby men because they think men want it, and in all this mutual babying it is forgotten that men and women are not babies but adult human beings who can find happiness only in the full use of their developed energies.

Yet, whatever the cause, woman at least has now come to a place where she is helpless unless man helps her. He must first help her, for she has so long been trained in the idea of her inferiority that it may be she has no initiative to make any fundamental change in herself. He, at least, is self-confident. And the only way he can help her is by demanding more of her. And where he must demand more of her is first and most in the home. Any American man who marries a vigorous, alert, well-educated girl, a girl eager and anxious to make a success of herself and of wifehood and motherhood, and lets her become the average woman she too often does become, is equally to blame with her. For woman is pathetically eager for man's approval, and far more than she should she patterns herself to his wish. I do not excuse man in his vanity about supporting his wife and paying all the bills, in his degenerating too often into sulkiness and irritability from fear of what people will think of him if she works outside the home, in his giving so little of his real self to his marriage and his home.

Man seldom helps woman. Yet it has suddenly become urgent that he do so, for unless he does he will lose woman altogether in the slave she will become and has become if democracy changes overnight into fascism. If American men value democracy, let them look not only to fifth columnists and pro-Nazi sympathizers. A greater threat to democracy than these lies in the way men think about women, in their ignorance of her true female nature, in their carelessness of her development, in their contempt for her great abilities, in their ignorance of her much-needed and now almost entirely lacking influence in the affairs of nation and world, an influence which if it were there would supply the balance which we have not now. Until woman contributes her share to all of life we shall not find the balance between men and women which will conserve life and improve life conditions. Only this balance can provide the true foundations for peace. We shall have no peace until men and women work together outside as well as inside the home, not because either is superior to the other, but because life is designed on such balance and evil results when the balance between the sexes is lost. It is not meaningless that the dictators have risen in countries where woman became subject.

We have in our country a pulling and hauling between national ages, the medievalism of women and the modernity of man. Between them is the child, emotionally pulled back by the mother, intellectually hauled forward by the father. How can we expect him to be a harmonious being? The average young American is not harmonious in himself. He is dazed, uncertain whether to be progressive or reactionary, his fine character and true idealism destroyed by this uncertainty; and he is bewildered as to its causes. And within her own self woman is both medieval and modern, and thus torn again. She is educated to be modern and then put back into traditional life. And man is full of impatience with her, not understanding why or what is the matter with her or what it is in God's name she wants, when it seems to him he is a sacrifice already to her whims —as too often, indeed, he is. He must realize that she does not now know what she wants and that it is he who must teach her what she is and what she can and ought to be to him and to the world.

But how can there be space for such comprehension of each other in the hurried hours of early morning and late evening? The day separates man and woman, and the separation has to be mended, and there is left to them only the night. How many marriages are begun with full determination for comradeship and equality, and how many are destroyed merely by the separation of man's day and woman's day and its inescapable consequences! And night cannot mend the separation, for night is not enough. The closest intimacy of flesh is not intimate enough for comradeship and equality, and when in desperation men and women try to make it enough, the flesh itself sickens and so all is lost.

No, the trouble with American men and women is that they do not live together. For the eternal triangle of life is not the two women and a man or the two men and a woman which novels and plays hold dear as the material of plot. The real triangle of life is made up of three equal sides, and they are man, woman, and child. And the perfect equilibrium of these three as individuals and the balance in their relation to each other makes up the true stuff of human life. It is a triangle in which all human beings are involved in one of the three ways at least, and usually in more than one. It is rare that the triangle is perfectly equilateral. More often one side is long and strong and the others short and weak, and then the triangle is an inharmonious thing. Sometimes two lines of it are equal, and the connecting third is dwarfed by them and it is still inharmonious. And yet the triangle of man, woman, and child ought to be equilateral, for only when it is are these three complete as individuals and complete as a whole.

3 . THE AMERICAN MAN

PHYSICALLY groomed and shaped to similarity by mass production of garments and general education and by that horror of anything which tends to draw attention to his looks or to seem finicking and peculiar which is a vestige of pioneer times, the American man is never happier than when he knows he is looking perfectly ordinary. But inside that carefully ordinary exterior there is astonishingly often an independent, thinking mind and a warm, though essentially prudent and conservative, heart. This prudence does not at all contradict a generosity seldom found anywhere else in the world, particularly toward women and children. American men enslave themselves not to their families, to whom as a matter of fact they give little time, but to their own impulses of generosity, which it seems they cannot restrain even for their own good.

The compound of this generosity is a matter for pondering. It is more than a simple wish to bestow goods upon the beloved. If it were the impulse only of devotion, such great love would make it impossible for a man to spend nine-tenths of his waking time away from those he loves so much. The American man sees less of his family than any other husband and father in the world, and accepts this separation with a tranquillity which ought to be alarming to woman but is not, for she bears it with equal tranquillity. This mutual tranquillity in accepting lives almost completely separate is only another proof of what seems to me to be a fact—that in our country men and women do not enjoy each other as much as they should, or else they would find more ways of being together.

Why, I have long asked myself, are American men so materially generous to their families? Why do millions of them spend their lives to give women and children—but especially women—every possible comfort and luxury? Why is it that when a man does not do this he immediately loses caste? Why do men take it for granted that women must have those comforts and luxuries? Is it true that women demand them, or are women ever given the choice between a man's time and companionship and his money?

These questions have no complete answer, of course. It would take a poll more delicate than any yet devised to answer them truthfully. Perhaps the truth is not so important—often it is not, if the effect of truth is evident and can be examined. Whatever the cause of this astounding generosity of men to women in providing material goods for them to the extent of devoting all their time and energies to the task, the effect is not so much of unselfish generosity as of generosity at a price. A price for what? A price for freedom from home and the responsibilities of rearing and training children. American children are reared almost entirely by women. Men excuse themselves from it as once they excused themselves from responsibility for conception. Actually they are as inexcusable in the one matter as in the other. They have an equal responsibility with women for the development of the children they beget. It sounds naïve and ignorant to say that they have not. So they say instead that they are too busy making a living for the family.

This masculine escape from the responsibility of children is the root of the so-called overfeminization of our American civilization about which men have hued and cried so loudly of late. I read these noisy he-man shouts with wonder at their illogicality. Who, pray, is at fault for this overfeminization? Women have had to do the best they can alone with the children. The inside of the average home is a place fairly familiar to us all, for most homes are alike. Man is not there, and woman copes with hearty, rebellious, demanding growing children almost entirely by herself. The whole day is·shaped toward peace if possible when man comes home. If it is simply not possible, man takes a loud, brief part in compelling it, not to train the children, but for his own peace and comfort. Woman pores alone over books of child care and goes off to hear lectures on adolescent psychology and avoids as far as possible annoying man with the problems of their children, partly for his sake, partly to shield the children from his sudden angers and commands, and partly because she seldom can make him understand the real problem and so cannot agree with his too-easy solution of it. The price man pays for his immunity from the cares of family life is his generosity in comfort and luxuries.

Of course, he gets his satisfaction out of this generosity, aside from irresponsiblity in the home. The measure of luxury in the making and maintenance of his home is the measure of his success as man—that is, the size of his income. Money in the bank is hidden, but it is splendidly displayed in a fine house, a good car, two if possible, and in fur coats, diamonds, and private schools. It is just as well displayed in a different stratum in a good Ford, an electric refrigerator, a set of overstuffed furniture in the parlor, and store clothes.

These are all good things. I shall never cease to feel the fine meaning in the sight of the parking space around the small factory in the village near which I live. I stop often and look at all those cars. The factory workers here come to work in their own cars. Our own hired man comes to work on the farm in his car every day. It is a wonderful, an exciting thing. I am used to a miserable line of human beings creeping into a Chinese factory at dawn, to come forth exhausted after dark, small children often among them. The children of our factory workers live in the healthy little village on top of the hill and play on tricycles and roller skates after they come roaring home from the neat schoolhouse. It is all infinitely better than factory life in China.

Still, I am not only thinking of the overfeminization of which our society has been accused. It is perfectly true that women do not see enough of men here, and that the children suffer from the lack of the influence of men upon them in home and school. But men lose more. They lose very much when they relegate home and children to women. They lose fun and the excitement of growing, developing life—life which they have had a part in creating. But they lose something deeper than that. They lose touch with the source of life itself, which is deep in the very process of living with a woman and the children a man has created with her. When he lives not there but in his office, in his work, among other men, he is strangling the roots of his own being. If he can comprehend fully the one woman and can help her to comprehend him, they are both fulfilled. When they enlarge this mutual comprehension to include children, then the universe is within their grasp and they cannot be disturbed. They have life in their time.

As it is, woman struggles to do her work and man's, too, in the home; and of course she fails. And when she fails, man is impatient with her, and she feels an inferior creature.

The truth is that women in America too easily accept the idea of their inferiority to men—if not actually, then in order to curry favor with men, who imagine it easier to live with inferiors than with equals.

I know quite well that any American man hearing this will laugh his usual tolerant laughter, though tolerant laughter is the easiest form of contempt. He always laughs tolerantly when the subject of a woman is broached, for that is the attitude in which he has been bred. And immaturely he judges the whole world of women by the only woman he knows at all—his wife. Nor does he often enough want the sort of wife at whom he cannot laugh tolerantly. I was once amazed to see a certain American man, intelligent, learned, and cultivated, prepare to marry for his second wife a woman as silly and unfit for him as the first one had been, whom he had just divorced at great expense and trouble. I had to exclaim before it was too late, "Why do you do the same thing over again? She's merely younger and prettier than the other one—that's all. And even those differences are only temporary." To which he growled, "I do not want a damned intelligent woman in the house when I come home at night. I want my mind to rest."

What he did not see, of course, though he found it out later, was that there could be no rest for him of any kind in such a woman as he had chosen. He was soon irritated by a thousand stupidities and follies and beaten in the end by his own cowardice. He died a score of years too soon, exhausted not by work but by nervous worry. His two wives go hardily on, both headed for a hundred, since he left them what is called "well provided for." Neither of them has ever done an honest day's work in her life, and he literally sacrificed his valuable life to keep them alive.

And yet, going home that day from his funeral and wondering how it could have been helped, I knew it could not have been helped. He was doomed to the unhappiness, or at least to the mediocre happiness, with which many if not most American men must be satisfied in their relationships

with their women. For if he had been married to an intelligent, superior woman he would have been yet more unhappy, since, with all his brilliance as a scientist, he belonged to that vast majority of American men who still repeat today the cry of traditional male pride, "I don't want
my wife to work." Which may also—I dare not say how
often—be translated, "I do not want my wife to be interested in anything except ME."

That is, he wanted a woman who would contain herself
docilely within four walls for him. With a stupid woman
he was bored, and yet he feared that an intelligent, energetic, educated woman could not be kept in four walls—
even satin-lined, diamond-studded walls—without discovering that it is still a prison cell and that sooner or
later the prisoner, even though with love and kisses, turns
upon the jailer.

For no home offers scope enough today for the trained
energies of an intelligent modern woman. Even children
are not enough. She may want them, need them and have
them, love them and enjoy them; but they are not enough
for her, even during the short time they must preoccupy
her. Nor is her husband, however dear and congenial,
enough for her. He may supply all her needs for human
companionship, but there is still more to life than that.
There is the individual life. Woman must feel herself
growing and becoming more and more complete as an individual as well as a wife and mother before she can even
be a good wife and mother. I heard a smug little gray-
haired yesterday's woman say not long ago, "No, I don't

know anything about politics. It takes all my time to be a good wife and mother. I haven't time to keep up with other things." Unfortunately, her husband, successful doctor that he is, has time to keep up not only with his practice and with being what she calls a "wonderful husband and father," but with another woman as well. But that, too, is one of the things she knows nothing about. Yet who can blame him? He is clever and full of interest in many things, and his wife is dulled with years of living in the four walls he put around her. It is a little unfair that he so encouraged her to stay in the walls that she came to believe in them completely as her place.

But tradition is very strong in this country of ours. We Americans are not a backward nation in the making and using of machines, but we are backward in our attitude toward our women. We still, morally if not physically, shut the door of her home on a woman. We say to her, "Your home ought to be enough for you if you are a nice woman. Your husband ought to be enough, and your children." If she says, "But they aren't enough—what shall I do?" we say, "Go and have a good time, that's a nice girl. Get yourself a new hat or something, or go to the matinee or join a bridge club. Don't worry your pretty head about what is not your business."

If she persists in being interested in things beyond her home we insist that she must be neglecting her home. If she still persists and makes a success through incredible dogged persistence, we laugh at her. We even sneer at her, and sometimes we treat her with unbelievable rudeness.

And yet, vicious circle that it is, I cannot blame Americans for distrusting the ability of their women. For if the intelligent woman obeys the voice of tradition and limits herself to the traditional four walls, she joins the vast ranks of the nervous, restless, average American woman whose whimsies torture her family, who spoils the good name of all women because she is often flighty, unreliable, without good judgment in affairs, and given to self-pity. In short, she becomes a neurotic—if not all the time, a good deal of the time. Without knowing it or meaning it, she falls too often to being a petty dictator in the home, a nagger to her husband and children, and often a gossip among her women friends. Too often she takes no interest in any matters of importance and refuses all responsibility in the community which she can avoid. She may be either a gad-about and extravagant, or she may turn into a recluse and pride herself on being a "home woman." Neither of these escapes deceives the discerning. When will American men learn that they cannot expect happiness with a wife who is not being allowed to develop her whole self? A restless, unfulfilled woman is not going to be a satisfied wife or satisfactory lover. It is not that "women are like that." Anyone would be "like that" if he were put into such circumstances—that is, trained and developed for opportunity later denied.

"Plenty of men are denied opportunity, too, nowadays," someone may murmur.

Yes, but the times have done it and not tradition. There is a difference. And one man has as good a chance as another to win or lose, even in hard times. But no woman has even a man's chance in hard times, or in any times.

I am not so naïve, however, as to believe that one sex is responsible for this unfortunate plight of too many American women. I do not believe there is any important difference between men and women—certainly not as much as there may be between one woman and another or one man and another. There are plenty of women—and men, for that matter—who would be completely fulfilled in being allowed to be as lazy as possible. If someone will ensconce them in a pleasant home and pay their bills they ask no more of life. It is quite all right for these men and women to live thus so long as fools can be found who will pay so much for nothing much in return. Gigolos, male and female, are to be found in every class and in the best of homes. But when a man does not want to be a gigolo he has the freedom to go out and work and create as well as he can. But a woman has not. Even if her individual husband lets her, tradition in society is against her.

For another thing we Americans cannot seem to believe or understand is that women—some women, any women, or, as I believe, most women—are able to be good wives, ardent lovers, excellent mothers, and yet be themselves in the world, too. It is true that as yet only the exceptional woman can accomplish this task, for man is not educated for fulfilling his responsibilities in the home. But did he take his responsibilities so that she could have only her own, we would see many more women living a rounded life to the benefit of everyone, both inside and outside the home.

That we do not as a matter of course allow her to do this seems strange, for as a nation we have fitted woman to be an individual as well as a woman by giving her a physical and mental education and a training superior to that of women in any other nation. But when she comes eagerly to life, ready to contribute her share not only to home but to government, science, and arts, we raise the old sickening cry of tradition, "This isn't your business! Woman's place is in the home," and we shut the door in her face.

I am aware that at this point American men here and there will be swearing and shouting, "You don't know what you're talking about! Why, we give our women more than any women on earth have!" With that I perfectly agree. American women are the most privileged in the world. They have all the privileges—far too many. They have so many privileges that a good many of them are utterly spoiled. They have privileges, but they have no equality. "Nobody keeps them back," the American man declares. Ah, nobody, but everybody! For they are kept back by tradition expressed through the prejudices not only of men but of stupid, unthinking, tradition-bound women. Here is what I heard a few days ago:

A young woman wanted a new book to read and her father offered to send it to her. "What do you want?" he asked.

"Anything, only not one by a woman," she said carelessly. "I have a prejudice against books written by women."

"Why?" she was asked.

"Oh, I dislike women," she said. What she really meant was that she despised women so much and with such jealousy that she actually disliked women who did anything beyond the traditional jobs that the average women do. There are thousands of women who uphold medieval tradition in America more heartily than do men, just as in China it is the ignorant, tradition-bound women who have clung to foot-binding for themselves and their daughters. No, women have many enemies among women. It goes back, of course, to the old jealous sense of general female inferiority. Tradition, if it binds one, should bind all, women feel.

Sometimes, I confess, I do not see how American men can endure some of their women—their imperiousness, their peevishness, their headstrongness, their utter selfishness, their smallness of mind and outlook, their lack of any sense of responsibility toward society, even to be pleasant. As for laziness—look at the motion picture houses, the theaters, the lecture halls, crowded all day with women! The average house, even with no servant, must be no full-time job or they could not be there in such hordes, they could not be there at all. But children go to school as soon as they stop being babies, and electricity cleans and washes the house and clothing, and husbands are away all day. So what is there for the restless woman to do? She goes to the show and comes home, if she has any sense, to wonder what life is for and to think that marriage is not so much, after all, though if she had not been married she would have been ashamed of herself. For tradition works there, too, and it would have made her seem, if unmarried, unsuccessful as a female.

"But what are we going to do?" the harassed American man cries. "There aren't enough jobs now to go round. And women are getting into industries more and more."

This in itself is nonsense and a masculine bugaboo, though merely getting a job is not what I mean. The truth is the number of women in industries is increasing at so slow a rate, and wars only temporarily quicken that rate, that it is shocking when one considers how long women have had an equal chance with men for education and training. In the last fifty years—that is, half a century during which education for women has enormously increased—the percentage of women in industry and the professions has increased from 14 per cent only to 22 per cent. That means millions of women have been made ready for work they either had no chance to do or never wanted to do.

As to what men are going to do with women, I do not pretend to know. But I know I have never seen in any country—and I have seen most of the countries of the world—such an unsatisfactory relationship between men and women as there is in America. No, not even in Japan, where women as a class are depressed as Chinese women never were. For even the Japanese are wiser in their treatment of women than we Americans are, though certainly far more severe than the more humane Chinese were. They keep women down from the beginning so that they never hope for or expect more than life is to give them. Japanese women are not restless or neurotic or despotic, nor are they spoiled children. They are patient and humble and resigned. They have not been trained for equality, and they do not expect it. Nor have they apparently the subtle powers for inner development that the Chinese women had. Japanese women know that they are upper servants, and they fulfill their duties gracefully and ably, and perhaps even thus are happier on the whole than women in America. To know what one can have and to do with it, being prepared for no more, is the basis of equilibrium.

No, what is wrong in America is the way we are educating women—that is, as long as things still are as they are, and life for the American woman is still controlled by old traditions. For men do think of women, if at all, in the old simple, traditional ways. Then women ought to be prepared for this sort of life and shaped through childhood and girlhood for what is to come. The root of the discontent in American women is that they are too well educated. What is the use of it? They do not need college educations nor even high school educations. What they ought to have is simple courses in reading, writing, and arithmetic, and advanced courses in cosmetics, bridge, sports, how to conduct a club meeting gracefully, how to be an attractive hostess, with or without servants, and how to deal with very young children in the home. This last course, obviously, should be purely optional.

But all this present higher education is unfortunate. It has led American women into having ideas which they can never realize when they come to maturity. A college education may, for instance, persuade a girl to become interested in biology, which may lead her into wanting to become a surgeon. And yet she will never have the chance to become a first-rate surgeon, however gifted she is by birth. People will not allow it; not only men but women will not allow it. They will look at her tentative little shingle and shrug their shoulders and say, "I don't feel I'd *trust* a woman surgeon as I would a man." So after a while, since she has to earn something, she takes her shingle down and accepts a secondary position in a hospital or a school or goes into baby-clinic work, supplemented by magazine articles on child care—or she just marries a surgeon. But inside herself she knows she still wants to be a surgeon, only she cannot. Tradition does not allow it.

Or a college education may lead a girl into wanting to be a banker. It is natural for women to be interested in finance, since they own about 70 per cent of America's money. But it is unfortunate if a woman thinks she can be a real banker. I have talked with a good many women who work in our American banking system. Not one is where she hoped to be when she began, and a very fair percentage are not where they should be with their high executive ability, or where they would be if they were men. As one of the most brilliant of them said to me bitterly, "I know if I were a man I would, at the age of fifty-five, and after thirty years of experience, be a bank president. But I'll never be anything but an assistant to a vice-president. I reached the top, for a woman, years ago. I'll never be allowed to go on."

A good deal is said, too, about the profession of teaching for women. There are a great many women teachers in America, many more in proportion to men than in other countries. The truth is that men here allow women to teach in lower schools because they themselves do not want to teach in anything less than a college. And even the best men do not like to teach in women's colleges nor in co-educational colleges. The finest teaching in America, I am told, is done by men for men.

As for the arts, I know very well that the odds are strongly against the woman. Granted an equally good product, the man is given the favor always. Women artists in any field are not taken as seriously as men, however serious their work. It is true that they often achieve high popular success. But this counts against them as artists. American men critics may often show some respect to a foreign woman artist, feeling that perhaps the foreign women are better than their own. But they cannot believe that anyone belonging to the species they see in department stores, in the subways and buses, or running to the movies and lectures, or even in their own homes, can amount to anything in the arts. Indeed, American men cannot think of a woman at all, but only of "women," so foreign is it to them to consider woman as an individual. And the pathetic effort of American women to improve their minds by reading and clubs have only heightened the ridicule and contempt in which their men hold them. For culture is not contained in what a person knows, but in what he is and does.

To educate women to think, therefore, so that they need the personal fulfillment of activity and participation in all parts of life is acute cruelty when they are not allowed this fulfillment. They should be educated not to think beyond the demands of simple household affairs or beyond the small arts and graces of pleasing men, who seem always to want mental rest. The present method is not only cruel, it is extremely wasteful. Good money is spent in teaching women to do things for which there will be no need. Men strain themselves to furnish educations for their daughters which the daughters would be happier without, and not only happier but better women because they would be more contented women.

It is not only wasteful but dangerous. To educate women as we do for our present state of traditionalism is to put new wine into old bottles. A good deal of ferment is going on. And if we keep this up, more will come of it. No one knows the effect upon children, for instance, of so many discontented women as mothers. Amiable, ignorant, bovine women make much better mothers than neurotic college graduates. And a woman does not need to complain aloud to let her children know she is unhappy. The atmosphere around her is gray with her secret discontent, and children live deprived of that essential gaiety in which they thrive as in sunshine. So few American women are really gay. This must have an effect.

So, though I am impressed with the fact that American women do not, as a group, seem happy, privileged as they are, I am not surprised. I know that happiness comes to an individual only as a result of personal fulfillment through complete functioning of all the energies and capabilities with which one is born, I do not for a moment mean that all women must go out and find jobs and "do something" outside the home. That would be as silly and general a mistake as our present general clinging to tradition. But they should be trained and ready to work anywhere that their capabilities lie. They should not be doomed by the accident of birth to a "sphere."

Let us face the fact that as a nation we are in a medieval state of mind about the place of women in society. Let each man ask himself—he need not answer aloud—where he really wants his woman. The majority, if they are honest, must acknowledge that they would like contented, adoring women who want no more than their homes. I do not quarrel with that. What is, is. All I say is, let us realize facts. Tradition rules the relation of the sexes in America. Women are not welcome outside the home except in subsidiary positions, doing, on the whole, things men do not want to do. The great injustice to women is in not recognizing this frankly and in not preparing them for it.

But of course there is the chimeralike possibility that we might change tradition. I do not see anyone capable of changing it unless men will. But they do not even want to talk about it. They do not want the woman question stirred up, having, as they say, "enough on their hands already." To them, of course, women "stirred up" simply means nervous, illogical, clamoring creatures who must be placated in one way or another. They cannot conceive of woman as a rational being equal to themselves and not always fundamentally connected with sex.

For, as has been truly said, emotionally many American men are adolescents, kind, delightful, charming adolescents. "He's just like a boy" seems to be considered a compliment to a man in America. It ought to be an insult. This horrible boyishness lingering on in persons who should be adult is as dismaying as mental retardation. It is responsible for our childish tendencies to "jazz things up," to "make whoopee," to think of being drunk, of removing "inhibitions," of playing the clown, as the only ways to have a good time, to the complete destruction of adult conversation and real wit and subtler humor. It certainly is responsible for wanting women to be nothing but wives, mothers, or leggy relaxations for tired business-men. Even a pretty college girl said despairingly not long ago in my presence, "You can't get anywhere with men if you show any brains. I have to make myself a nit-wit if I want dates. Oh, well, that's the way men are!" There are too many nice and rather sad American women who patiently accept even their middle-aged and old men as perennial "boys." "Men are like that," they say, at least as often as men say, "Women are like that."

And how often do women tell each other that a wife must be a mother, too, to the husband! In secret truth no self-respecting woman wants to be a mother to her mate. She longs for the equality of adulthood between them. Another woman has been her husband's mother. It is repellent to her, or should be, to take that place. There is something very faulty in the relationship between man and woman when the mate in woman must be subdued to the mother. And certainly this perpetual mothering degrades the man and hinders his development into his fullest manhood.

Nothing could show a greater misunderstanding between men and women than this frequent fatalistic remark, therefore, that one or the other is "like that." Neither men nor women are like that, if "that" means what they now seem to each other—childish, misunderstanding, fundamentally uncomprehending of each other's needs and natures. With such attitudes, how can men and women enjoy each other? They meet stiffly for social functions, drink together in an earnest effort to feel less inhibited, play the fool guardedly, and feel queer about it afterward. Or they meet for physical sex relations in the home or out. And they jog along in family life. Of the delights of exploring each other's differing but equally important personalities and points of view, of the pleasure of real mutual comprehension and appreciation and companionship there is almost none. Tradition decrees that after marriage real companionship between persons of opposite sex must cease except between husband and wife.

Tradition decrees that all companionship, indeed, between men and women is tinged with sex. Such an idea as interest in each other as persons aside from physical sex is almost unknown. Women, talking of this among themselves, say, "Men don't want anything else."

I am inclined to think they are right. The average American man demands amazingly little from his women, nothing much except to look as pretty as possible on as little money as possible, to run the home economically with as little trouble as possible to the man when he comes home tired. What educated, intelligent, clever, gifted woman is going to be satisfied with that? What average woman would be satisfied, even? Ask the average man if he would change places with a woman, any woman—the idea horrifies him! Yet women are far more like him than he knows or wants to know, and modern times have done everything to make her so.

No, our men, perennial boys, too many of them, will not do anything about changing tradition. They do not know how, absorbed as they are in the games of business and war, abashed as they are in the presence of sex as anything except simply physical, and afraid as they are of women. They are, naturally, afraid of women, or they would not cling so to tradition. They were afraid of their mothers when they were children—their imperious, discontented mothers—and that fear carries over into fear of their wives and fear of all women, in industry as well as at home. It leads to the attitude of petty deception which so many perennially boyish men maintain toward their women. It led them long ago to invent chivalry, and by that admirably clever chicanery to remove women from all possible competition with men as human beings by making them into angels. Incidentally—or was it incidentally?—chivalry made a solemn duty for men the boyish pursuits they best loved: tournaments, processions, jousts and battles, and dressing up in armor and plumes. What were the Crusades themselves but a fine chance to get away from responsibilities at home and to go gallivanting off to foreign countries? It had to be made a holy war, of course, to make men feel right about it and to convince women that it was all God's will. Women would never have let men go if it had not somehow been made a matter of conscience for them to do it.

So, naturally enough, men do not want women "getting too smart." I heard a carpenter working in my home say pontifically to his assistant about to be married, "And why would you want a woman eddicated? I says if I want eddication I can go to the public library. A woman should know just so much as when it rains she stands on the sheltered side of the street. It's enough." And after a moment he added solemnly, "You don't want a woman what can talk smart. You want one what can keep quiet smart."

The voice of America's perennial boys, I thought, speaking out in a carpenter, but heard as clearly in the embarrassed reserves of an after-dinner circle in a drawing room. And yet I do not blame them. There are so many women who chatter without thought, who stop all attempts at conversation with continual commonplaces uttered with all the petty authority of ignorance. And the fetters of chivalry, once so gaily worn, today hang heavily upon American men. Foolish, haughty women, standing in crowded buses, staring at a tired man in a seat, accepting favors as their right; peevish, idle women, wasting their husbands' money; dogmatic women talking ignorantly about practical important matters—men must try to be polite to them all alike. I do not blame American men for anything except for not seeing that not all women are the same—yes, and for not seeing what women could be.

We are so clever with machines, we Americans. But we have done a silly thing with our women. We have put modern high-powered engines into old, antiquated vehicles. It is no wonder the thing is not working. And there are only two courses to follow if we do want it to work: we must go back to the old simple one-horse-power engine, or else we must change the body to suit the engine—one or the other. If the first, then tradition must be held to from the moment a woman is born, not, as it now is, clamped upon her when, after a free and extraordinarily equal childhood and girlhood with boys, she attempts to enter into a free and equal adult life with men and finds it denied her, to discover then that her education has had nothing to do with her life. Either she must not be educated for freedom or else we must be willing to let her go on to being free. This means that American men must cease being "sweet boys" and must grow up emotionally as well as physically and face women as adult men. But they, poor things, have not been fitted for that either! Besides, of course they are afraid of what women might do. And women, inexperienced and eager, will probably do as many foolish things as men have until they have had as much practice.

Of one thing I am sure, however: there will be no real content among American women unless they are made and kept more ignorant, or unless they are given equal opportunity with men to use what they have been taught. And American men will not be really happy until their women are.

4. THE AMERICAN WOMAN

AMERICAN women among others are not born all alike, whatever they achieve in this respect afterward. By nature they seem, indeed, among other possible classifications, to fall into three groups. The first is the talented women, or women with a natural vocation. This group is, naturally, a small one, for the women who are in it must have, besides their talent, an unusual energy which drives them, in spite of shelter and privilege, to exercise their own powers. Like talented men, they are single-minded creatures, and they cannot sink into idleness, nor fritter away life and time, nor endure discontent. They possess that rarest gift, integrity of purpose; and they can work, day upon day, mentally and spiritually as well as physically, upon the one necessity. Such women sacrifice, without knowing they do, what many other women hold dear—amusement, society, play of one kind or another—to choose solitude and profound thinking and feeling, and at last final expression.

"To what end?" another woman may ask. To the end, perhaps, of science—science which has given us light and speed and health and comfort and lifted us out of physical savagery; to the end, perhaps, of art—art which has lifted us out of mental and spiritual savagery.

I remark, however, in passing that it is notable in the United States when a woman of this talented group chooses to spare herself nothing of the labor which a similarly talented man performs for the same ends— though why should it be notable, unless perhaps it is because we are accustomed to expect so little from a woman?

The second group of women is, though far larger than this first one, yet like it in having a vocation; but here it is the vocation of the home. In this group is the woman who is really completely satisfied mentally and spiritually with the physical routine of motherhood and the activity of housekeeping. When her children grow up she begins again with her grandchildren. Her brain, literally, has been encompassed by the four walls of her home, and is engrossed and satisfied with its enclosed activities. As long as her four walls stand she is contented, busy, useful—a sweet, comforting, essential creature who perfectly fulfills her being and her function, who brings nothing but simple happiness to those about her, though only so long as she gives them freedom to come and go as they will and does not limit them by her own simplicity.

But both of these, the woman born talented and the woman born domestic, may be dismissed from mind. Their combined number in proportion to the whole number of women is very small, and in the second place they are safe and stable citizens, since they know what they want to do and are doing it—in short, they are contented, and any contented person is safe and relatively sane.

There remains the last group, a very large one, for in this are the rest of the women; and these are the ones I call the gunpowder women. Here are all of America's millions of women who are not compelled to earn money to keep from starvation, who have no definite talent or vocation, who have only a normal interest in home and children, so that when these are adequately tended they still have surplus time, energy, and ability which they do not know how to use. To make conditions more difficult for them, they have usually a fair or even an excellent education and brains good enough at least to be aware of discontent.

It is the gunpowder women who suffer most under the burden of privilege which American women have been given to bear.

I set this sentence alone because the cause for the existence of these gunpowder women is this heritage of privilege which so oppresses American woman. The talented woman can ignore oppression and go on doing what she was made to do, as man does. And a born housekeeper, if her disposition is amiable—as, thank God, it more often is than not—is a comforting and comfortable soul who cannot be spoiled by privilege since she is happy in her work. But here is this other and far more frequent woman, able, free, educated, who quite often really wants to contribute something directly to her world and not merely through husband and children. She seldom can, however. Privilege denies it—she is so privileged that her world makes no demand upon her. More than this, no one even expects anything of her. Her very friends discourage her, though they be her fellows in discontent. If she tries tentatively to do something a little more serious than her fellows are doing they cry at her, "My dear, aren't you *wonderful!*" meaning, "Why on earth do you do it?" meaning, "Aren't you queer?" meaning, "You think you're smart!" meaning, indeed, all those things which discontented, helpless women do mean when they see one of their number behaving as the rest of them do not and being therefore a reproach to those who do nothing.

For the vicious result of privilege is that the creature who receives it becomes incapacitated by it as by a disease. Privilege is a serious misfortune anywhere, and the more serious because American women do not realize that the privilege they boast is really their handicap and not their blessing. I am sure they do not realize it because in the agreement and disagreement I have had with what I have written about this, nearly all the women said, reproachfully if they disagreed, "You seem to forget that women in America are the most privileged on earth," and apologetically if they agreed, "Of course, I know women in America are the most privileged on earth, but—"

And every time this was said, in either fashion, a certain bit of Chinese history came warningly into my mind. This is the history:

Centuries ago, when astute China was about to be conquered by the naïve and childlike though physically

79

stronger Manchu, the Chinese used a weapon which gave them the final and actual victory, though the Manchus never knew it. When they were conquered, the Chinese said in effect to the Manchus, "You are our superiors. Therefore we will perform all unpleasant tasks for you. You shall live in palaces apart, and there enjoy yourselves. Sums of money will be set aside for you. You need not labor or strive. We will do everything for you. We want you only to be happy and enjoy yourselves."

The Manchus were delighted with this. They laid aside their weapons, went joyfully to the fine palaces the Chinese gave them, and began to spend their lives in pleasure. In a short time the Chinese were ruling their own country again, as they always had, and the Manchus were as good as dead. Easy food and drink and plenty of leisure had reduced them to complete ineffectuality, just as the Chinese had planned it.

Now, therefore, whenever I hear an American woman begin brightly, "Well, anyway, we are the most privileged—" I remember the Manchus and am troubled. There is something too sinister in this matter of privilege. And yet it is true—I cannot deny it, though I wish I could—the women of the United States are the most privileged in the world. We have never even had a very serious struggle to achieve our privileges, at least any struggle comparable to that of women in other enlightened countries. Privileges have been bestowed upon us, thanks largely to the inflated value which pioneer times gave to American women. That inflation still lasts, although happily it is decreasing. For the moment when American women hit what commercially is called an all-time low, they will be forced to wake up, and then perhaps they will put an honest value on themselves as human beings, and thus the struggle which other women have made or are making will begin and the result ought to be valuable to everybody. But that moment has not yet arrived, and meanwhile women go on under the handicap of privilege.

Of course, many women in other countries, not understanding any more than we do the effect of unearned privilege, envy American women. I suppose hundreds of Oriental women have said to me at one time or another, "How lucky you are to be an American woman! You have freedom and equality with men. Your parents do not groan when you are born, and your brothers do not look down on you as less than they. You can go to school. You need not even marry if you do not wish to—at least you need never marry someone you do not like."

I agreed to all of this, and I still agree to it. I had rather be an American woman than a woman of any other country in the world, not because of anything we have, but because everything lies ahead of us still, as women. But if I had a chance now at those Oriental women, after these years spent among my own countrywomen, I would answer something like this:

"It's true we are very free. We can be anything we like, we American women—lawyers, doctors, artists, scientists, engineers, anything. But, somehow, we are not!"

"You're not!" the Oriental woman would say, astonished. "Why not? Do you mean the doors are open and you don't go out?"

"Well, we go out—" I would have to acknowledge. "I suppose most of us go out in some sort of work, if we don't marry first; but we secretly hope to marry first so that we need not, or we want to work just a year or two and then come back into the home and shut the door and be secure in the old way."

"Don't you want to be independent, to be free to come and go as you like?" the Oriental woman cries. "Ah, if I could support myself, know I need not obey father, mother, husband, son—all my life—"

"Oh, we American women don't obey anyone," I tell her quickly. "Our husbands support us in the home, but we don't obey them. We do come and go as we like. Of course, we work in our own way at house and children, and for a few years we are even quite busy. But we have a great many ways to save labor, and the schools take our children early, and then we have a great deal of leisure— at least, *you* would think us very leisured."

"Then what do you do?" the Oriental woman asks blankly.

"Some of us work, the rest of us amuse ourselves some- how," I reply.

"Women are fed and clothed for that?" she asks.

"Yes," I reply. "Many of us—"

She cannot understand this, and indeed it is difficult to understand, and I cannot explain it to her. Why, in a country where everything is free to women and women are so privileged, is it remarkable when a woman is first-rate in anything? But it is. Thanks to our privileges, which compel us to no effort, it is the truth that men excel us, numerically as well as actually, at everything except child-bearing, and doubtless if men had to bear children they would soon find some better way of doing it. And women, seeing themselves outstripped without understanding why they are, and yet feeling themselves as able as men, grow discontented and join the crowded ranks of the gun-powder women.

The home, of course, has been the stronghold of this privilege. Behind its sheltering walls too many women have taken full advantage of every privilege—the privilege of security, the privilege of noncompetitive work, the privilege of privacy. Yes, of privileges women have had plenty, and yet most of them have been denied the one great blessing of man's life—the necessity to go out into the world and earn their bread directly. And this one blessing is worth all privileges put together, for by it man has been compelled to put forth his utmost effort, whetting his brain and sharpening his ambition; and so he has accomplished much.

For Nature is not unjust. She does not steal into the womb and like an evil fairy give her good gifts secretly to men and deny them to women. Men and women are born free and equal in ability and brain. The injustice begins after birth. The man is taught that he must develop himself and work, lest he and his woman starve. But the woman is taught merely to develop such things as will

83

please the man, lest she starve because he does not want to feed her. Because of this one simple, overwhelming fact, men have been the producers, the rulers, and even the artists.

For necessity makes artists, too. Many a talent is born without its mate, energy, and so comes to nothing unless energy is somehow created to develop the talent. Necessity is the magic of this creation for the man, for if he has talent he will, if driven desperately enough, apply his compelled energy to his talent and become at least a fair artist—for genius still remains the combination of highest natural talent and highest natural energy of a quality which functions without outside stimulus or compulsion.

"But," a gunpowder woman retorted to this yesterday, "a man can combine his talent with his breadwinning." She looked around the walls of her comfortable prison. I could feel her thinking, "If I had been free, I might have been a great painter."

To which I retorted, "How do you know it is not as easy to combine housekeeping and art as it is to make art a business? You have never tried it because you have never had to."

No, the man is lucky. By compulsion of society and public opinion, if he has any ability and pride he simply must work. Nothing excuses him. Home cannot be his escape. And in desperation he somehow begins to try to make a living by what he wants to do. And whether he succeeds or fails in it, he has no refuge from work, hard and endless and full of insecurity. He bears, indeed, the brunt of that heaviest load of all—insecurity.

The curse of women has been that they have this privilege of refuge in the home. Behind closed doors they may or must work, it is true, but according to their own hours and ways. They escape all the discipline of concentration upon one task, often uncongenial, hour after hour, year after year, the mental discipline of hard creative thinking, the ruthless discipline of social organization. I have been both breadwinner and housekeeper, and I know that breadwinning is infinitely more tedious, more taxing, more nerve-racking than housekeeping. Indeed, cooking, cleaning, caring for children, if you know necessary bills are pretty certainly going to be paid, is almost a soporific and as good as play after the insecurity of competition in business and the arts. For safe in the home a woman becomes used to flitting from one thing to another, and her mind forgets or never learns how to concentrate or perhaps to work at all. There, leaning upon another's efforts, she becomes lazy—if not physically lazy, lazy in that core of her being which is the source of life and development so that when her children are grown, and in a few years they are, and her mechanical tasks are over, she is fit for nothing more. She has excused herself from a life of labor because of these short-lived tasks which, necessary as they are for a time, should never have been considered adequate for her whole self.

The truth is that, although women are needed today in every sort of life in the United States, they do not even see that they are needed. So many women have become so corrupted by privilege that they stare out on events and conditions around them with the same unseeing, lackluster eyes with which Hindu women have looked out of the windows of their zenanas. The Hindu woman was not educated, and she could not pass out of her door uncovered, and this American woman is free to come and go, and she has been given what education she wanted; and yet there is the same look of defeat in her eyes that there is in the Indian woman's. Neither is fulfilling that for which she was born, but the American's discontent is keener because she knows it, whether she will acknowledge it or not; and the more clever she is, the more educated, the more of a gunpowder woman she is.

I do not in the least blame her for being a gunpowder woman. I can only sympathize with all her small daily explosions, her restlessness, her irritability, her silliness, her running after this and that in heroes, in arts, in clothes, in love, in amusements, her secret cynicism and her childish romanticism, her fears and her little explosions, too, of daring, which accomplish so little because they never go far enough. She is unpredictable, not from a calculated charm, but because she really does not know what to do with her inner self.

And why should she know? Why should so much more be demanded of her, if she does anything, than is demanded of a man? A man is educated and turned out to work. But a woman is educated—and turned out to grass. The wonder is not that she is unpredictable but that she is not insane. Nothing is arranged for her as it is arranged for the man, who, under the rule of society, by a series of efforts combined with ability has his life laid out for him. I say that if a gunpowder woman with no boss to tell her what to do, with no office to schedule her days and force her to activity, with no financial necessity compelling her, no creative demand driving her, no social approbation urging her—if this woman can be her own taskmaster and fulfill herself by some accomplishment, then she is a creature almost superhuman. It is too much to ask of her very often, and when she achieves something she ought to be greatly praised.

For consider, please, the advantage a man has in our country over a woman. I repeat, for it is the key to all his success: a man must work or he starves. If he does not actually starve, at least society looks down upon him and makes him ashamed. But a woman within her home may live an absolutely idle existence without starving and without being despised for it. Yet an idle woman ought to be despised as much as an idle man for the good and happiness of all women if nothing else. Anyone who takes food and clothing and shelter for granted, even though it is given by one who loves to give it, and makes no return except privately to an individual, ought to be despised. A woman owes something to the society which gives her husband a chance to earn for her, and social pressure should compel her to make that return.

And yet this woman has not even the help of that social pressure. Society pays no attention to her so long as she "behaves herself" and stays at home. She is that most unfortunate of persons, idle because nothing is demanded or expected of her, and yet unable to be happy because she is idle. No wonder discontent is her atmosphere, that discontent which a visitor from Europe once said when he landed in the United States struck him like a hot wind. What is discontent but spiritual gunpowder of the fullest inflammability? Only the stupid woman can avoid it.

When I consider this handicap of privilege, then, which has produced these gunpowder women in my country, I cannot find a single word of blame for them. I know that men would never have risen to their present pre-eminence in all fields if they had had such a handicap—if, in short, they had not had the advantage of the compulsory discipline of work. I am sure that men would behave certainly no better than women if, after the wife was off to office and the children to school, the man were left alone in the house. If he could sit down and read a mystery story at ten o'clock in the morning he, too, would do so, although a busy world hummed about him. He would curl his hair or waste an hour on his fingernails if there were no one to tell him it was not the time for that sort of thing. He would, it is true, have as she does a deadline to meet in the late afternoon, but with no one to check on him to see how time-wasting he was in getting there, he would waste as much time. He could even be as poor a housekeeper as she sometimes is, and no one would blame him very much. His wife would merely work a little harder so as to be able to hire a cook. No, without the discipline of regular labor, of fixed hours, of competitive standards, the man would be where the woman is now. If women excel in nothing, therefore, it is at bottom as simple as this and not because men's brains are better than women's.

It is a pity, for these gunpowder women are as much a lost source of power in the nation as are the flood waters that rise and rush over the land to no useful purpose. Spoiled, petty, restless, idle, they are our nation's greatest unused resource—good brains going to waste in bridge and movies and lectures and dull gossip, instead of constructively applied to the nation's need of them.

"What can we do about it," some of them cry at me, "if that's the way things are?"

"Nothing," is my reply. "Nothing at all, unless it happens you also want to do something. Nobody will make you do anything. It all depends on how much of a self-starter you are whether you can overcome your handicap or not. Nobody will help you to set about finding out what you want to be or help you to be it. For I don't want to stress doing something as much as *being* what you want to be. Mere activity is the occupation of monkeys and lunatics. Still, unfortunately, doing and being are very closely tied together, and unless you are doing what you secretly want to do, you aren't able to be the sort of person you want to be."

Yet perhaps it is too much to demand of women that, without any help or encouragement—and, indeed, often with active discouragement and ridicule—they put aside privilege and take their place in the world's work as ordinary human beings. The Manchus could not do it. They, too, went on helplessly living in their palaces and houses, and then one day the Chinese realized there was no use in feeding them any more since they were no use to anybody, and so they put them all to death in a quiet, matter-of-fact way, and that was the end of Manchus in China.

Of course, exactly that will not happen to women anywhere unless some too-enterprising scientist succeeds in creating life without the help of the female. Women would then doubtless have a very hard time convincing the invincible male that there was any real reason for their further existence. But I hope that long before then the gunpowder women will have come to such a unified state of combustion that they will refuse to tolerate their condition of privilege any longer out of sheer boredom.

For the vital difference between the privileged Manchu and the privileged American woman is that the clever Chinese allowed the Manchu no modern education. He was born into his ivory tower and never left it. But the privileged American woman enters hers when she reaches her majority, and she takes with her the influences and the memories of a world in which she had a vital part in her youth and school years, and consequently she never becomes quite tame. If education improves enough, or if society suddenly develops a new need for women, the gunpowder may work more quickly than it is working now merely through the medium of individual discontent.

The best thing, of course, that could happen to American women would be to have some real privation and suffering come upon us because we are women, instead of all this privilege. But we have had no such suffering and are not likely to have any. Everything has been too easy for us and is too easy now. We do not feel the wrongs of others because we have never been severely wronged, except by all these privileges.

As things are, the only real hope for the progress of women generally is in those women who, because of some personal necessity, do work and take an active share in the life of the world, and who are participants and not parasites. The working woman—may her numbers increase!—will not perhaps ever fight for women, but perhaps she will fight to right a wrong near her, and by her work at least all women are brought more actively into the life of the world.

For I am convinced there is no way of progress for women except the way men have gone—the way of work or starve, work or be disgraced. A good many women are plodding, willingly or unwillingly, along that way, learning to take what they get and do with it, to live with hazard and competition, to push past failure and begin again, to keep their mouths shut instead of spilling over into talk or a good childish cry—in other words, they are becoming mature individuals in their own right.

It is a hard road for long-privileged creatures, and one is alternately amused and angry to see many of them avoiding it and retreating again into the home. The newest generation of women, frightened by the realities of depression and economic struggle, are clamoring afresh for marriage and the home, and today marriage competition is keener than ever. Women's interest in work and a profession has not been lower in the last half century than it is now. Indeed, it seems that women, having seen a glimpse of reality in the depression years, are in definite, full retreat into the safety of femininity, into the easy old ways of living to please one man, and catching him and persuading him to do the work for two. Mind you, there are ways and places and times when a woman can find a full job in her home. But to one such woman there are fifty who do not and cannot, and there is no use in pretending they are earning their keep as human beings.

"Why work if I don't have to?" someone asks. Well, why not, if not simply to see if women do not feel happier, as men do, in using all faculties and capabilities? I am always glad when I hear a woman has to work to earn her own living. I scorn the usual talk, "Poor thing, she has to go out and work after all these years of being provided for!" Who gave anyone the right of being provided for all those years when everywhere in the world people have to work? Yet this is not the important thing. The real point upon which a woman is to be congratulated when she does have to work is that at last compulsion is upon her to exert her body and mind to its utmost, so that she may know what real fatigue is and honest exhaustion and the salutary fear that maybe she is not good enough for the job which brings her bread, and, above all, that she may know the final inexpressible joy of complete self-forgetfulness which comes only in soul-fulfilling work.

Work is the one supreme privilege which too many women in America, with all their extraordinary unearned privileges, never know. And yet it is the one privilege which will really make them free.

I am uncomfortably aware of women who will cry out at me when they read this, "Why don't you tell us what to do? It is easy enough to say something is wrong, but the useful thing is to say what will right it."

To which I answer: Nothing will right it for everybody at once or, for some women, ever. The most tragic person in our civilization is the middle-aged woman whose duties in the home are finished, whose children are gone, and who is in her mental and physical prime and yet feels there is no more need for her. She should have begun years before to plan for this part of her life. Her mind at least should have been working toward it all the times when her hands were busy. It is as difficult for her to begin something now in middle life as it would be for a middle-aged man to change his profession. How can she re-educate herself at fifty?

And yet I do not know that she is more piteous than the many young women, educated for nothing in particular, who now out of school are trying to find out what they are for. For the most part, of course, they occupy themselves in the enormously competitive marriage business which they carry on, unaided, in spite of their inexperience. If they marry, they follow the path the fifty-year-old woman has gone and arrive at the same dead end. The gunpowder group is made up of all of them, young and old.

93

"But what can we do?" When they are pricked, thus they bleed.

Well, what can women do in the United States, women who do not have to do anything and who can, if they will, do anything? The question seems idle, a mere evasion, in the face of the condition of the world today. If man, conditioned to war, cannot provide a society which sees war at its beginnings and stifles it, can woman not try at least to help him here? Is she forever to go on blindly giving birth to sons that men may go on blindly killing them off? There is a possibility of a better sort of life than this, but to it she gives no thought. It is easier to breed, as beasts do, careless of what befalls the progeny.

And who said men's brains are better at politics and government than women's? A few weeks ago an able woman, working for her political party, sat in my office and told me disconsolately that women were given only petty offices in the party, assistant something-or-other, vice-presidencies on small committees, where their only duty was to obey the man above them.

Why should obstetricians be men, or dentists or scientists or architects? I have heard a famous gynecologist say that gynecology could never be perfected until women entered the field seriously, for no man could ever understand completely what childbearing was or a woman's needs at that time.

Business has been built basically without the constructive hands of women. If women had not been so hidden in the home we might never have had this accursed relation between capital and labor.

But her influence has everywhere been lacking. Whatever has developed in the life of the nation has developed without her brains and her effort. I do not put much stock in this matter of her inspiration of man in his home. It seems not to have had much actual effect. He has done as he wanted to do, with or without it. I suspect woman's inspiration of man has been a good deal of what men call "kidding the little woman along." How can one inspire when one does not understand through participation?

Of course, if women's work in the nation has scarcely begun, I am too much of a realist to believe that, were it all done, the nation would be completely changed for the better. Some things would be better and some might be worse. The great change would not be in what women accomplished. It would be in the women themselves—that is, the gunpowder women. The talented woman and the homemaker would be about as they are. Nothing will change them much. But the gunpowder women would no longer be fussing and fretting. Their energies would be happily released elsewhere than on harassed husbands and overwrought children.

And I refuse to be too cynical. I believe the whole nation would be better off if women would do the work waiting for them to do, not only because these women themselves would be happier and their relations with men more satisfying than they now are. I believe that by using the brains now idle and the energy now disintegrating in that idleness, women could immeasurably improve all conditions in our country, if they would. It is perfect nonsense for any woman to ask what there is for her to do. There is everything for her to do. If she wants a small job, let her look around her village or her neighborhood. If she wants a big job, let her look around her state or think as largely as her nation, or even realize that there is a world beyond. Not to see the infinite number of things to be done is to prove the damage that privilege does to the perceptions; not to do after she sees is to prove the damage already done to the will.

Is it hopeless? For the women resigned to privilege it is hopeless—for these women who give up even discontent and so pass into nothing. It is not necessary to give them a group to themselves. Having died to life, they simply await burial.

But for the gunpowder women there is every hope. I listen to their discontent with all the excitement and delight that a doctor feels when he hears the murmur and feels the beat of an uncertain heart, however fluttering and unstable, beneath his instrument. I know this, at least —as long as a woman complains, she is a gunpowder woman, and still alive.

And yet who can blame man if it is the gunpowder woman who makes him feel there are too many women in his world?

5. MONOGAMY

POLYGAMY is, of course, ubiquitous, for it is the only solution men have yet found to the problem of too many women. There is no country in the world without polygamy. So far the only question has been whether it is to be recognized or not. The Western people have on the whole decided it should not be recognized, and the Eastern people have decided that it should. France was a compromise between these two points of view, of which the United States is one extreme and China the other.

Curiously, I cannot think of a point upon which the ideas of these two peoples, the American and the Chinese, are further apart than upon this point of polygamy. Otherwise we are much alike. Our geographical environments being so similar, we have, in spite of the wide difference in the space of our two histories, developed into amazingly similar peoples, which is doubtless the reason why we instinctively like each other. But in this matter of recognizing polygamy we are opposite. Americans are furiously shocked at the idea of a man's having legally more than one wife at a time. Chinese are equally shocked at the idea of the illegitimate children of whom we have so large a number. To the Chinese it is repulsive and immoral for society to visit upon a helpless child the punishment due to adults.

This difference in point of view upon polygamy comes from many causes. There is the Puritanism still rampant in Americans, though subdued and denied, and the naturalism which long human experience has given to the Chinese. There is the romanticism in the Americans, still young and demanding love as an essential to marriage, and there is the realistic common sense of the Chinese, who by now are born old, and who know what the young will not acknowledge—that romantic love does not last. There is, moreover, a love of liberty in the abstract in American men which forces them to compromise with themselves to the extent of allowing their women to have with them equal education and opportunity, though they are often angry if women make use or take any advantage of their education and opportunity, and the Chinese practicality which says calmly that everybody is better married and, since polygamy is the only way that everybody can be married, it is better to make polygamy legal so that all children can be born equal in status and with equal claims of inheritance, and since polygamy and the equality of women with men are incompatible, the equality had better be given up.

To say that either point of view is right and the other wrong is impossible. Each has its evil and its good, and it depends upon point of view as to whether evil or good weighs more heavily, as the modern Chinese are beginning to discover in their first efforts toward monogamy.

For monogamy in modern China has not been any more successful than it has been in other countries—that is, it has not been successful at all if one means by monogamy every man's having only one wife at a time. In China, of course, there were peculiar difficulties. Polygamy for forty centuries cannot be changed overnight into monogamy. There were hangovers, and one of them was the old-fashioned wife. For with the revolution in China came a new vision to men and women of each other as equals. They longed for companionship with each other as equals, a companionship neither had had under the old system. It is a hunger as old as the Garden of Eden and as new as today. The best among men and women of any race in any time dream of this companionship and know by instinct that only in such companionship can each be made whole.

But when monogamy was made law in new China a whole generation of young men and women, though in the full romance of their youth, were already too old for it. They were married or betrothed, and betrothal in old China was as sacred as marriage, and these bonds were suddenly hateful. Young men ardent in the revolution were thrown with young women made free by equal ardor in a great cause. And though many were already parents, how could they fail to feel the demands of a love which they had never felt before?

And in that time of transition, divorce seemed cruel, though it was made easy and private. There had been no need for divorce under the old system, for if a man's heart changed, he simply enlarged his household by another woman. The first wife kept her place and position in the family. Nowhere was she displaced except in the most intimate relations to the man, and that society ignored. But when monogamy came the man did not even want her in the house. These two, modern man and modern woman, wanted to be alone.

Those were days of heartbreak. Good women, young and old, were made homeless by monogamy. They were disgraced, they had nowhere to go and no place in society, and their children were motherless or, if they took them away, then fatherless. Many men were not ruthless enough and could not inflict the suffering upon their families necessary for monogamy. Nor were young women willing enough to be cruel. There was compromise. Old-fashioned wives "went to the country," and there was no public divorce, though these poor souls were widowed, for modern love would not allow their husbands to visit them any more. So they lived apart, thousands of them, victims of the revolution and mourning the security and kindness of polygamy.

But there came another problem. Centuries of polygamy had had its effect upon men and women. It had created in them two different attitudes of mind toward each other. It had given woman a feeling of indissolubility in her relationship with man, but to man it had given superficiality in his relationship to woman as an individual. He could not take woman as seriously as she took him. She had never been his whole life, as he had been hers. And this superficiality was native to him. With the best wish in the world toward one woman, the Chinese man found it difficult to think in terms of one woman when there were women everywhere around him. In some desperation Chinese women tried to be as modern as they thought they were, and the result was for a time a sort of monogamy that had all the evils of polygamy with none of its benefits. Men and women were sexually promiscuous and superficial in their emotions toward each other. Family life suffered disastrously, for the old was gone and the new not established. The security, economic and emotional, which polygamy gives to the whole, if not to individuals, was lost. Moral standards were gone between men and women because the definitions of good behavior were gone and conscience destroyed.

The result of this was the loss of happiness. Men and women were terrified by their unhappiness together, and just before the war there was a definite return to old ways, not permanently but that the transition might be made less roughly and with less disaster. Parents were beginning to assume again a modified responsibility toward the marriage of their sons and daughters, without the old arbitrary method of arranging betrothals without acquaintance between the betrothed, but still without the new freedom of free mingling of the sexes and falling in love. For, as one famous Chinese has put it, it is a folly that at the one time in life when man and woman have the least ability to reason—namely, when they are in love—they should take the most important step in life—namely, marriage.

Compromise, therefore, was the order of that day. The wisdom of the parents, it was said, should combine with the wishes of the children. Parents know their children better than the children know themselves. They should guide and persuade, at the same time accepting the child's refusal. It was a civilized compromise.

What war has done to that phase of a changing civilization cannot yet be known. There are other things more demanding in China today even than marriage. There is the simple necessity of remaining alive. Men and women are working side by side on the battlefield, in industry, in schools and hospitals. They are having a sort of companionship they have never had before. Equality has been forced upon both, not by the demand of either but by the necessity of keeping each other alive. What will happen afterward, who can say? But still I do not see the old polygamy as a relationship possible to them any more. There will be another way, and if it is successful monogamy it will be because this experience they are having together has educated them for each other.

For the reason that monogamy has not been entirely successful so far in any country where it has been tried is that men and women have not been educated for it equally. Monogamy is a word lightly pronounced, an idea accepted by many people as only decent; and yet no civilization has been sufficiently advanced in democracy to achieve it actually as well as legally. For only under a complete democracy is monogamy possible on practical grounds, unless some means can be devised to limit the number of women.

China tried for centuries to limit women by allowing girls to be killed at birth without considering it murder. Still there were too many women to achieve monogamy. Even the hardships, always greater than men's, which women have had to endure, the hazards of childbirth, tremendously increased by ignorance, were not sufficient in China. In spite of all this, for centuries enough Chinese women survived in proportion to men to allow for one woman to every man, and enough surplus women to provide for polygamy.

This is very discouraging. The resistance and toughness of women are embarrassing and complicate greatly all problems of the relationship between men and women. What shall be done with the inevitable surplus women if it is true that women belong in the home? So far monogamy has not been able to provide homes enough. When any American man begins the familiar growl of sending woman back to the home, where to his way of thinking she belongs, let him pause and consider where the home is to come from and who is to provide it. For to carry out that ancient scheme of every woman in a home, legalized polygamy will be a necessity. Monogamy can never provide a home for every woman.

Even polygamy alone cannot stretch to such enormous provision—it will have to be helped by compulsory marriage. In the United States the population is still balanced enough so that the ratio of women to men is about equal, though this may not be true as time goes on. Men are destroying the balance even now by refusing to marry or by delaying marriage, and every time a man refuses to marry, even in God's country there is a surplus woman. Men cannot enjoy the liberty to marry or not as they please which they now enjoy in Western countries and still talk about woman's place being in the home. It would be pleasant for them to be able to enjoy such liberty with none of the consequent cares; but pleasure, unfortunately, always has a price. In this case the price is surplus women, restless, inquiring, eager, keen of mind, strong of body, demanding of their life some worth—surely a disturbing price to any peaceful, liberty-loving man!

I have only once seen polygamy attempted on any large scale by an American, though in his own fashion every married man who has extra-marital relations is a secret polygamist. But Mr. Jones tried to regularize polygamy and make it decent. I feel sure his motives were good and even kind. I knew Mr. Jones as a small mild-looking traveling salesman of household soaps. He made too little to support his family, though he traveled five days a week urging his soaps upon the people of our rather conservative farming region. Mrs. Jones was a sweet-faced, dark-eyed young woman, and there was a two-year-old baby girl, and besides her the expectation of a son soon to arrive. It was a happy little family, and I know them because Mrs. Jones helped out the budget by doing odd jobs of sewing and washing for us.

One morning when the three of them were sitting at breakfast together in their little bungalow the door opened, and two policemen walked in. Mr. Jones knew at once what was the matter. He wiped the egg off his mustache, rose and said affectionately to his wife, "Nellie, I'm wanted for bigamy."

Mrs. Jones, telling me of it, said she knew at once that he was guilty, even though he was the best of husbands and as moral a man as could be found, a church-goer, and one who never so much as glanced at a girl's ankles even on the street.

"How did you know?" I inquired.

"He was a very accommodatin' man," she said sadly.

And so it seemed he was, for when all was revealed the total was not two wives but three, with a grand total of nine children born and two expected. In his circuit Mr. Jones had divided his week regularly between his three homes. He had supported none of them wholly. Each wife had worked to help him out.

His wives were all good women. They met together to discuss their common problem after Mr. Jones was settled in jail, and they talked with frankness and sense. All agreed that Mr. Jones was a good man and that it was not his fault. It was the old problem of the surplus woman. These women wanted homes of their own. They were eager to be put back into the home. Many women are. Nine out of ten women working for their own bread today are longing to be put back into the home. Mr. Jones, being an accommodating man, yielded to the demand. Each woman said honestly that she had "led him on." When all had been revealed, the two younger women looked at each other and agreed to give him up to the first Mrs. Jones, who was after all the oldest and had five of the total of children. The last I heard those two were actually contributing to her support while Mr. Jones was serving his sentence. It is a long one, and he is still in jail. All of the women feel there is something unfair about it, though they do not exactly know what. As the third Mrs. Jones said to me with vague distress in her pretty eyes, "There's something wrong somewheres when after all nobody meant any harm."

What she means is that they were all obeying perfectly decent instincts. Mr. Jones was not a libertine, and none of the women were wanton. They would not for anything have knowingly borne illegitimate children. The proper words had been said over all of them. As for Mr. Jones, the few times I saw him he seemed a man full of a gentle resigned philosophy. Probably he believed that women did belong in the home and had already decided rightly that monogamy could never achieve it. In his own way he was therefore not only a reasonable man but a practical man and a pioneer, a real benefit to society; and to put him in jail has been no solution either to his own problem or to the problem of surplus women as a whole. Indeed, as the little Mrs. Jones I know said, "We'd all have ruther gone on the way we was, without knowin'. After all, we had our homes, and now we haven't nothin'."

No, the only way to make of monogamy a practical accomplishment is to make of marriage a possibility but not a necessity. Woman must give up the futile notion that some man will certainly ask her to marry him and realize

106

that nowadays a good many women are never asked. Many good women and even some pretty ones never have the chance to get back to the home, and if monogamy goes on their number will increase. The only sensible course, therefore, is to educate women into independent human beings, ready to take their place in the work of nation and world, and to educate men in allowing them to do that work. For the only other alternative is polygamy, the recognized and legal polygamy of the East or the furtive American polygamy of illegal relationship which brings Mr. Jones to jail and leaves three women again homeless and a large number of children illegitimate.

As things now are, it is woman who makes some sort of polygamy necessary when she demands marriage as her only real happiness and work, and at the same time makes of marriage such a heavy economic burden that modern man grows despondent. The slightly skeptical look habitual to the American man whenever he contemplates woman is the outward sign of his inward question, "Is she worth it?" In all fairness, it can scarcely be answered that she is. Much that she used to do is now done. Even laundries will darn and mend, and home cooking is to be found at the lowest possible rates in public eating places. Perhaps woman herself realizes her slight practical worth to man, and that is why she tries to make up her weight in charm, like a very small present tied up in fine ribbons. Unfortunately, a little charm goes a long way, usually too long, before she knows it. This is her predicament. She must create new values in herself for man.

How? I suppose by finding out if she can be what he really wants. That may be impossible, for it is doubtful if a man knows what he wants inside a woman any more than outside. He likes, however, a good ensemble; and at present woman's inner ensemble is too often composed largely of scraps—scraps she has heard from her mother, scraps that women tell her in secret, scraps she reads from women's pages in magazine and newspaper, scraps she gets in lecture halls and movies. She is lucky if she has any spiritual and mental ensemble whatever.

Would marriage be worth having if it were between two human beings who were equals and who had like responsibilities toward themselves and society, and if it were no longer economic escape for the woman? It would have some advantages for the man, at least. He could be sure that the woman loved him for himself and did not accept him for the sake of a home and security from breadwinning for herself. He could feel that he had a partner and not a dependent. If he fell ill or the times were bad, she could carry the family more easily than she does now. Moreover, if she were educated as a responsible and independent human being, he need not be harried by a false pride, as he now is, in being ashamed to have his wife work lest people think him unable to provide for her. Marriage would be a finer relationship between man and woman if it could be separated from false social standards and economic benefit and the degradation which such benefit brings to the one who receives it and the one who gives it, too.

And what a relief it would be to woman to have the burden of necessary marriage taken from her! How fine a thing she might make of marriage if she could choose it and not be compelled to it for economic support or social standing! And sweet would be her liberty if she could fall happily in love without fearing that if she chooses home she must give up a work she enjoys and is trained for; if, like man, she could know that life and love were big enough for both home and work, and the dreadful choice, so glibly and foolishly expressed in the phrase "home or career" need not be forced upon her, if by nothing else than by the censure and self-satisfaction of other women limited in their own abilities. If economic pressure and social stigma had nothing to do with marriage for woman, we would have the possibility of real monogamy at last, and the only possibility.

But the American man needs education for monogamy as much as the woman does. Like the Chinese man, polygamy has become more or less instinctive to him. He does not often attempt to solve a national problem as bravely as Mr. Jones did, but in his secret heart he is not often willing to allow woman an equal place beside him outside the home, and when he is not he prevents monogamy by compelling women to marriage as their only resource. The reason for his reluctance is, I suspect, partly because he is afraid it might mean an equal place beside her in the home. He knows somebody has to keep the house clean and look after the children, and if his wife helps with the work outside, he will have to help with the work inside, and when he comes home he does not want to be bothered. There are men to whom this is the chief objection to allowing women out of the home. They would not mind having women work outside, but it stands to reason they cannot work both inside and outside at the same time. Many of them have to, of course, but the result is satisfactory to no one, and women must be educated out of attempting such impossibilities.

But deeper still in the heart of man is his desire to be pre-eminent in the management of the world. When we get down to the bone, this is the truth.

6. WOMEN AS ANGELS

DEMOCRACY is not to be confused with liberty, nor the love of democracy with the love of liberty. Who does not wish to be free and who does not love liberty? But democracy is another matter. Our forefathers founded the nation on love of liberty. It is doubtful whether they understood much about democracy. If they did, it was to envisage it in terms of individual liberty.

But democracy is not individual liberty. It is very nearly the opposite of that. There must be serious curtailment of individual liberty in a true democracy. Whole groups of people must submit themselves to the decisions of the majority. Every four years even in our imperfect democracy such groups must resign themselves to an order directed by a person they do not want and controlled by policies they disapprove. They endure it because they have the hope and the machinery for change, and these are the great strengths of the democratic form of government. It provides for the revolutionary instincts of the human race, just as freedom of speech provides for the need for individual liberty. So long as a person can say what he thinks and feels when he is impelled to express his ideas and emotions, he will allow himself to postpone action. To speak, to criticize, has been a safety valve.

Do we want a real democracy? There will have to be some vast changes if we do. Negro Americans, for instance, would have to be given real equality with white Americans. No one can give them this equality to the point of removing race prejudice from the minds of ignorant and insensitive persons; but the government at least would have to recognize the equality of all Americans with each other, and it would, if we were a thorough-going democracy, be compelled to remove all discrimination against the Negro. Thus there would have to be forbidden the Jim Crow color lines wherever they are found. They are undemocratic and would have to be declared illegal. Hotels, restaurants, theaters, churches—all public institutions would have to allow everyone equal place regardless of color. Wages would have to depend upon ability and skill, and not upon color. And restricted areas in real estate could not exist.

But prejudice against colored blood is only one of the most obviously undemocratic aspects of our life. To say, therefore, that we are ready to fight to preserve democracy is not accurate, because we can scarcely fight for something we do not yet have. We are ready to fight, rather, to keep what we have—a national life of our own. It is a confused, contradictory, quarrelsome sort of life, and it cannot be called wholly one thing or the other; but it is ours and it is worth defending because it holds in it the possibility of change. We have not finished with ourselves yet, and we know it. The final pattern is not clear. If the white, Gentile, adult male believes that his nation is a democracy, let him remember that there are others—and perhaps nearer to him than he knows or cares to believe—to whom he appears only as a dictator. Free Englishmen see the face of their country in all the glorious brightness of democracy, but who can believe that in India the people, poor and oppressed, and kept ignorant and divided, can thus see the face of England?

To the Negro American the white American is a dictator and to the East Indian the Englishman is a dictator; and let us not pretend in our two great nations that we have not in our own selves the foul thing we would destroy elsewhere. There is only one thing more foul, and it is hypocrisy. And yet we have that hope which, when the crisis comes, will make the Negro and the East Indian fight on our side, or at least not against us. It is the hope, the possibility, of change. This is the germinal atom of democracy in us. Whether that germ is to grow and to bear flower and fruit depends on whether we are true men and women or hypocrites. Can we, will we, go on to real democracy, or will we let democracy remain a seed in the soil of our love of liberty? But a seed must grow or it will die, and seedless soil is barren earth, its potentialities unused.

Now love of liberty is the natural soil for democracy, and the only place where it can grow. It is right and inevitable that out of an individual's love for his own liberty should shape gradually the divine notion of democracy.

The process is simple enough. I love liberty and I must
have liberty, says one; and he takes it. But I also, says
another. Then do those two look at each other, measur-
ing and in doubt. Can two be free? Will not the freedom
of one forbid the freedom of the other? Weak and strong,
they look at each other. The way of the dictator is for the
strong to push the weak aside and maintain his own
liberty intact. The way of democracy is for the strong to
perceive that the love of liberty is in anyone, in the weak
as in the strong, and he allows that liberty. When one
encroaches upon the other, as he must, then the point is
found and fixed where liberty is greatest for each and its
sacrifices least to both. This point we may call democracy.

Individuals have found it, but as yet no nation. Within
all nations the strong still insist upon their liberty being
the larger. The difference is only in degree and change.
In fascism there is no mechanism for change, and liberty
belongs only to the rulers. In our country we allow for
change, and the degree of liberty is changeable, but the
point of democracy has not been reached because we are
not willing to reach it. Neither the strong nor the weak
are willing to reach it. That is, the strong do not recognize
the necessity of yielding up their greater liberty to the
point necessary to establish democracy, and the weak do
not realize the necessity of developing themselves to the
point of being able to use liberty. When I say strong in
America, I mean fundamentally the white, Gentile, adult
male and besides him those not economically depressed.
When I say weak, I mean women, Negroes, Jews, and be-

sides these all economically depressed persons. In every
country the strong and the weak are different persons, and
the only similarity is that in every country the strong are
numerically a small group and the weak are many. The
strong have another advantage anywhere. They have a
solidarity which the weak have not. The dominant race,
the male sex, power over money—these the strong always
have. Even when, as in the United States, women actually
own most of the money, yet their ignorance of how to use
it puts the power over it into the hands of men.

But the weak have no solidarity. Of many races, vari-
ously handicapped, they are a motley crowd. They have
nothing in common except their weakness and their help-
lessness, and this is increased by their division. They do
not often help each other. They try, each for himself, to
win against the strong, or to insinuate themselves with the
strong, hopeful each for his own benefit. And yet only in
the union of the weak can there be any real strength. As
it is now, the strong by their very strength are not ready
for democracy, and the weak by their weakness are not
ready for it.

Thus in the United States neither man nor woman is
ready for democracy—man by reason of his strength and
woman by reason of her weakness. When I say they are
not ready, I mean neither is willing to discover that jewel
point where liberties will meet and the balance of liberty
for both be found which is true democracy. For at that
point man must give up his most precious possession: the
belief in his own superiority merely because he is male. It

is time he gave it up, of course, as a practical matter. Science tells us all that there is no proof of any sort to be found that sex alone determines superiority. But facts never had anything to do with human beliefs. A three-year-old son of mine one day, as he contemplated an engine, pointed to the sand dome.

"Smoke comes out of that," he said.

"Smoke," I said, "comes out of the smokestack."

He turned large, calm blue eyes upon me. "I want to believe smoke comes out of the sand dome," he said tranquilly, and believed it.

He is the male of the human race. In a democracy he will have to acknowledge, however, that smoke does come, actually, only from the smokestack, and that his belief has nothing whatever to do with the truth.

How to get him to that point is, of course, another matter. He will not arrive at it except by two means: his own intelligence from within, which alone may lead him to want to know the truth, and coercion from without on the part of woman, developing in her turn to the point of democracy. Since intelligence to the point of wanting the truth is rare, coercion may have to go on and do its work.

That is, provided woman can perceive what she has to give up for democracy. What she has to give up will be her present privileges, the privilege of remaining ignorant in spite of education, the privilege of mental laziness, of not having to think thoroughly through anything because she knows the ultimate decision will not rest on her, the privilege of being willful and capricious and irresponsible, the privilege of idleness and of having time to spend lavishly on self-adornment and amusement, and the privilege of escape from the problems of the world, which are now the real problems of life, by retiring from them into her home and considering that her whole duty is there. She has, in short, to become an adult creature ready for the responsibilities of liberty.

But first of all she must want liberty, and this she does not now. I am asked, "What is the chief difference between modern Chinese and modern American women?" It is this: that modern women in China passionately love liberty and modern women in our country do not. There is reason for the difference. Behind the walls of home the Chinese woman has dreamed of freedom to go beyond them and, starved by ignorance, she has hungered for education. When at last freedom was given her she had already grown to the measure of freedom and could not have enough of it. Will she ever have enough of it? Will the time come when that remembered life of walls and ignorance will seem sweet to her and safe? I think not. I feel sure, never. For she will remember other things, too. She will remember the long monotony of her days, the emptiness of a mind that many trifles, however heaped, could not fill. She will remember the oppression upon her of inequality with man so that never, even in love, did she feel the joy of equality; and above all she will remember the loneliness that was hers as a human being in that scheme which forbade her companionship in work with man, her natural companion. And she, having been for centuries prepared for freedom, will not turn from it.

But woman in America is different. She has had liberty given her in a way peculiarly unfortunate. She was given it with too much else one day on a Christmas tree. It was handed to her tied up in red ribbons among many other beribboned gifts. Some of those gifts were courtesy and deference and all the mixed candies and fruits of chivalry which have bred in her an incurable taste for sweets. She was given a halo, too, to wear in her hair to make her look like an angel, and that she found so becoming she has never been willing to put it aside. She was given a blue ribbon for being the best mother, and a prize for being the best cook, and even a trip somewhere for being the best average woman. In a handsome leather-bound volume she was given the right to an education, and she was given a ticket to anywhere. She could come and go as she liked. She was given so many privileges that who can blame her if she overlooked the fact that a certain plain diamond, not set in anything, just a solitary hard pure diamond, was not there? But it was worth everything else put together. It was real equality with man in marriage and work.

She has begun to notice the lack now, for without that one thing she can make full use of nothing, not even of her liberty. For what is the use of courtesy that will not allow her to grow to her full powers if it interferes with man's place in work and government, and what is the use of having an education if it cannot be used to fulfill its purpose but must be kept as a toy for dilettantism? What is the use of being the best mother in a contest if she cannot be the best woman she is able to be? Why have liberty at all when she has nowhere to go? But, having been handed all the sweets of liberty, she is surfeited and has no taste for bread and butter, that solid plain fare of work and responsibility which, had she had to labor for it as Chinese women did, would have satisfied and fed her and made the sweets sweeter.

Now she wants to go back. Afraid of the responsibilities of true liberty, she is in retreat. Home, she says, home is her place. When she says this, it is not because there is enough for her to do there nowadays. When a woman stays in the home today she stays there most of her life alone. Modern industry takes man away from home most of the hours of his day and most of the years of his life, and modern education takes the child away. So home is a place for about half the women in our country at least, where woman has food and clothes and leisure, which is leisure however indignantly she denies it and shows her little engagement pad to prove how busy she is—that sorry list of luncheons and games and knitting and hairdressing and movies and shopping that are all that statistics tell us 45 per cent of our women have to call life! Well, at any rate, she can sit and play with her toys there and put on her halo.

American women generally do not want freedom. Amazing, terrifying that this is so; and yet one is constrained to believe it true. Else why their retreat? Why have they not moved simply and naturally forward to do

their work in the world beside men? Why are they un.
comfortable and ashamed when they are not married,
though the system under which we live does not provide
for compulsory marriage and how else can every woman
be married? Why are so few American women professional
in their attitude toward work? Why do they rush to give
up work and retreat when they succeed in securing marriage and a home? Marriage ought not to be a retreat from
work but stimulation to new work because, emotional
stability being thus established, the mind is really ready
for work at last. Why is it that American women inherit
some sort of curious medieval conscience about working
outside the home and never feel really right with God
until they can say, "I am devoting myself to my home"?

I cannot pretend to answer these questions. But the
answer has something to do with that halo. I know it because I see that women never look really contented without their halos, and they wear them whether they are
actually becoming or not. Why? Because men once long
ago gave those halos to women and told them that when
they wore them they looked divine.

The prejudice against women who dare to remove those
halos is more articulate at this moment than it has ever
been in the history of our nation. We are charged anew
with being out of our place. The cry again today is that
we must be returned to the home, taken out of industry
except in small subordinate or wartime jobs, and above
all taken out of public life and politics. We are charged
with weakening the nation, with being a pernicious in-

fluence upon men, who, it seems, are not strong enough to withstand us. If we are not actually harmful in public life, at least we do not improve anything. Nothing is better in government for our being there, we are told, so why should we be there? We only clutter up the offices and we are a nuisance. We must be removed.

Not only in America is this rumbling going on today. The new Vichy government in France has also decided to remove women. In fallen France the number of women who may be used in any industry is to be restricted. Women are to be eliminated altogether from government bureaus. And yet surely woman in France had achieved the utmost in femininity. For generations merely to murmur "Frenchwoman" has brought visions of charm and style to men and women alike, the difference being only that to men the vision had excitement and to women it was slightly jaundiced with jealousy. Woman in France had achieved the high point of compromise with polygamy. Marriage was acknowledged to be her right, and for it she paid the price of allowing polygamy to man as long as it did not shake her possession of his name and property. France did in the French fashion what China did in the Chinese fashion, but the Chinese way was more honorable, more just to woman and child, more decent for man.

But all the price that woman paid in France and all her charm and femininity were not enough. Wife and mistress, she falls back with the German *Hausfrau,* and bears besides the blame of man's weakness and degeneration and so the blame of France's fall.

Yet before American women get angry at the plight of women abroad we ought to examine our own situation. Intelligent women are all more or less conscious not so much of change here as of the slow tentative spread of an atmosphere which allows the open expression of opinions toward woman which before fascism came into being abroad would scarcely have been spoken aloud and in public places or printed on authoritative pages. A good many women are discussing the matter and are trying to find an intelligent solution for the problem before it grows any more acute. They must recognize that there is, of course, much truth in what is being said about women. The charge that feminization weakens the fiber of a nation is true. Feminization weakens anybody it touches, women as well as men. That it happens to be called feminization is comment on the place of women. It has nothing to do with being female. Men do well now to be alarmed by feminization, especially after those distressing stories from France. There is a terrible and evil power in the femininized, and men ought to fear it and try to keep it within bounds, because it is their own weakness made flesh in women. History is full of the tragedy of one man after another who has prevailed against armies but has not been able to prevail against one feminized creature, because to prevail against her meant to prevail against his own deep and unconquerable weakness. Who knows but that Hitler's secret lies in his own inner impregnability?

Whence came this feminine creature? She began in man's dreaming. Somewhere on the uneven road that men and women have jogged along together through the ages, they came to a fork to the left. The sign post on it read, "To Heaven." They stopped, plunged into indecision. The rough road ahead was unmarked and made no promises. Neither man nor woman knew where it had begun or where it would end, but to travel it was their daily life. But man was the incurable dreamer then that he is now. "Heaven," he mused. "I've heard fine things about that place. It's full of angels."

The woman said nothing. She was by nature a practical, hard-headed creature who did with what the man brought her. Some days she had so much she did not know what to do with it all, and on other days she had nothing. She struggled with this major problem of their family life in two ways: she learned how to preserve meat, and she scolded the man about his tendency to dream. Dreaming, she had discovered, was what made the food supply irregular. On days when something started him dreaming he forgot to hunt, and he came home empty-handed. She saw the glimmer of a dream now in his eyes as he looked up the road to Heaven.

"Let's keep on going the way we know," she said firmly. "We might not like Heaven."

"I'd like to see an angel," he said with longing. He looked at the woman and saw what he had sometimes noticed before: that she was plain. She was dusty and hot, and her hair was tangled. The dream in his eyes deepened.

"I've always heard," he said, "that angels are beautiful."

"I suppose you wish I were an angel," she said angrily. "As if I had time to sit around combing my hair and playing a harp!"

She was, of course, mixing up mermaids and angels, but they were mixed up in her mind. Whenever the road led by the sea, the man's eyes grew dreamy, too. To her the sea was a huge body of water full of dangerous waves and edible creatures. Her mind was on the possibility of eluding one and catching the other. She often stopped to hunt crabs and find oysters, especially if the man was having one of his dream days and looked for mermaids.

"Come on," she said now, "the children are waiting for us."

So she took him by the hand and she led him past the road to Heaven. She was a practical creature, tough and hard and secretly unsentimental, and persistence was her weapon. From the day of her creation she had been thus, for she had to do with birth and death and food and shelter and all the constant work of necessary things. She had no time to dream, and she had never learned how to do it. She had no need for Heaven, for she was perfectly happy as she was.

But she knew uneasily that this was not true of the man. Where he got this habit of dreaming she did not know, but he had always had it. Perhaps the freedom of his life gave it to him, the long hours of roaming in shadowy forests alone or with other men as free as himself. Now merely to drag him past the entrance to Heaven was not to make him free from the danger of his desire.

And so she found it as time went on. For, unable to discover what angels really were, he went on dreaming about them; and out of this came an idea so foolish, so sentimental, so mad, that when the woman first heard of it she merely laughed. It was simply this: that she make herself into an angel for him.

"Then, you see," he explained with luminous eyes, "I'd have an angel in my home. You would be my inspiration. I could dream about you."

She stopped laughing abruptly. She had an idea of her own. If she secured his dreams to herself instead of having them wandering over earth and heaven, would not all her troubles be solved? He would then always come home to her, and away from her he would be guided by his worship of her. For once something practical might come of a dream of his. But she was still a little cautious, never having seen an angel herself.

"What would I have to do?" she asked.

"Be beautiful," he said rapturously. "Be lovely and pure and good and gentle. Stay at home and make your skin soft and white and be always waiting for me when I come back."

"But if you don't bring home the meat?"

"I will, always, if I know you are dependent on me alone," he said. "To feel your dependence will bring out the best in me."

She said no more at the time but after thinking it all

over she decided she would try it, and from then on she tried to become an angel—that is, what the man thought an angel was, for he had never seen one either, so that to her being an angel meant simply that she struggled to be what he wanted her to be.

That struggle has now gone on for ages. It is a criss-cross, twofold sort of struggle in which woman fights not man but herself. For secretly she never really wanted to be an angel. She loves practical life, its hurly-burly and come-and-go, its strife and struggle and success and failure, and all that goes to make the everyday world. She watches man go off to that world in the morning with pangs of envy. But angels, he still tells her, cannot go into the world without losing their angelic qualities. Indeed, the man says to her as he kisses her good-by in the morning, "I like to think of you as being safe at home, my angel."

She smiles at him in the way she has learned he thinks is most angelic. But the moment he is gone she stops being an angel. She yawns, saunters about the house, does what she has to do when she has to, for being an angel has demoralized her and she does not work as she once worked. She talks over the back fence with other angels, brings her fingernails to a state of high perfection, reads in feminine magazines what angels are wearing this year and how they are doing their hair and what are the latest tricks angels use in charming men, and is nevertheless on the whole a good deal bored with the whole business.

But she does nothing about it, bored or not. For the effect of being an angel for centuries was that long ago

woman began to think she was an angel and then to believe that being a woman and an angel were the same
thing. When that complete falsity appeared to her as
truth, she became a creature so befogged about her real
being, so lost in the mists of man's legend about her, that
today she has no knowledge of what she is or ought to be.
The world has marched on while she has been out of it.
Today as an angel she is an absurdity, and she knows it,
and yet she has been an angel for so long now that she
does not know how to stop. Her crown is tarnished and
askew, her wings are useless and merely ornamental, since
she never goes anywhere on them, and her whole appear-
ance is antiquated; but, still, what else can she do but
go on being an angel? She is trained for nothing else.

There is no denying that women now present a some-
what ridiculous aspect as the result of all this. They are
neither women nor angels nor human beings. They cling
rather pathetically to the viewpoint of angels, though they
know it is out of date, for they are loath to give up both
the security of being angels and the confidence it gives
them of their moral superiority. And we women of this
generation are suffering most acutely of all because of this
reluctance. Our mothers made a foolish mistake in trying
to gain their rights as human beings without giving up
the privileges of being angels. There was that laughable
business of the female vote, for instance. The old angels
actually gave as one of their arguments for women to vote
that women would purify politics and uplift, by their
angelic qualities, the affairs of men. The poor creatures

had been told so often by men that they had these up-
lifting qualities that they believed it at last themselves
and thought that merely by their presence they would
uplift, as angels must.

It was a complete confusion between women and angels,
and now women can never live down the folly of it. They
should have demanded their rights as persons and forgotten themselves as angels. Angels have no place in politics or practical life. They are a nuisance, and they im-
pede progress. Men have to remember to take off their
hats to them and be polite to them and give up their seats
to them and not curse and swear and spit and loaf where
they are. Angels are sensitive creatures, moreover, accustomed to their own perfection, and they cannot take the
criticism that people must take when they enter active
and public life; and whenever they are foolish and incompetent, as angels usually are when they are out of
place, they do not want to be told so. When they are so
told, they develop nerves and temperament. The truth
is that heaven is their home and they ought to stay in it.
They should never have asked for the vote nor got it.
Angels ought not now to be allowed jobs outside their
homes, and certainly they should not be given public
offices.

But women are another matter entirely. They ought to
have the vote, not because they will purify or better anything, but because they ought to have it. Why should they
make anything better of politics than men have? There is
no more obligation upon them to do so. Any woman not

bemused and befuddled out of her senses by all this nonsense of being an angel would have known in the beginning that woman in politics would behave as other human beings do, and moreover that she ought to assert her right so to behave. She should have said, "I will have the vote and anything else there is merely because I, too, am a human being."

Of course, if she secured rights as a human being it would be dishonest of her to claim privileges as an angel. Here is still woman's greatest mistake. She wants to be human, but she does not want to give up the privileges of an angel. It would be wrong if I pretended that in this matter women at the moment are anything like unanimous. They are not. There are many women—perhaps an increasing number, perhaps not—who hate angels and will have nothing to do with being angels. There are others who love being angels, first, because they cannot bear to think they are not, but also because it is the easiest way to get their bills paid and so they will not give up being angels, only furbishing themselves up to look as modern as possible. There are plenty of men who like angels, and so angels still have their reward. And just at the moment they are feeling triumphant, for both Hitler and Mussolini are bringing angels back into fashion again, and we have always taken our fashions from abroad. And, lastly, there are the young females who cannot decide whether to walk out of their eggshells as women or to flutter forth as angels. They are waiting to see what men think they want just now.

It is absurd and laughable and touching and tragic beyond any tragedy, and men are not helping women at all
in their predicament. Men are impatient and scornful and
critical of women today as they never have been, as they
ought not to be, for they were properly to blame in the
first place for the present ridiculousness of women. What
business had men to dream of angels? What business to
dream at all? The absurdities and inconsistencies of life
in all our world have come from dreaming men. A man
dreamed that by dying on a cross he could save sinners.
But the world is full of sinners. A man dreamed that the
strong ought to bear the burdens of the weak. But the
weak are oppressed now as never before. A man dreamed
of a country where all would be free and equal, and for
many there is neither freedom nor equality. A man
dreamed of slaves set free by a stroke of the pen at the end
of a bitter war, and today the children of these slaves
suffer indignities and injustices untold because their skins
are black and for them there is still no freedom. A man
dreamed of communism, and in the name of communism
there is an oppression more horrible and more cruel because of the dream never made true. A man dreamed of a
society of nations where the weak could be free to live
and the strong would not oppress them, and today as
never before the weak are despoiled and the strong are
tyrants.

It is this eternal dreaming that ruins the world because
dreams are only dreams and men will not make them
come true. Man the dreamer, sentimental, unstable, emo-

tional, impractical, is unable to make his dreams come true, and because of this the world is in turmoil. Either man ought to dream more largely so that his dream can encompass reality, or he ought to be practical as woman is, who, if she seldom dreams, does not consider a dream complete unless it accomplishes her purpose.

There is a sense in which man has suffered more than woman from his own impractical dreaming. Because woman has allowed him to dream of her as an angel, because she has let him put her aside into a shrine, he has lost her. Our nation is effeminate from false femininity created by man. The balance and benefit which woman should have given she has not given. Women have become useless as human beings because of it. The devastating effects of man's sentimental worship and her isolation as its result have weakened her whole being so that what was moral worth in her has become self-righteousness, and what was capacity for honest emotion has become only capacity for sentimentality, and what was sturdy and independent and reasoning has become a cringing, crying insistence on angelic privileges. And now man does not like what she has become, though he forgets it all began with his wanting an angel of his own on earth, and he is no longer inspired by her, and her attempts to "uplift" him he finds only disgusting. For all of which he cannot be blamed, except that he is fundamentally blamable. Through centuries he has defined femininity and compelled women to be feminine by the strong force of his disapproval founded always upon his economic power over her.

This is the real injustice of men toward women, and it is so appalling that women cannot escape dangerous bitterness except by one comfort. It is that such injustice may compel women to reconsider their whole position and to give up the folly of trying to be angels any longer and so begin in earnest the task of being women. They have lost valuable centuries which cannot be retrieved. Against this loss they will have to work as men have never worked. They will have to destroy the whole angelic tradition, not only among men but in themselves, by repudiating all that is angelic. Women are not better than men. They should not be, they must not be, for the good of men and women in their life together. Women are not even naturally more delicate than men nor more "spiritual-minded" nor less human in any way than men are. Such notions still come from the angel tradition. Women are practical, hard-working, sensible, ordinary human beings. They are by nature less sentimental and less romantic than men. They are skeptical, often to cynicism. They are fearless, literal-minded, and tough in soul. They dislike and distrust all dreams, as well they may. Whether they will ever recover sufficiently from the evil they have suffered from men's idle dreaming cannot be prophesied, but if they do they will be careful not to dream beyond their power of performance, and the world could do with a little of that.

But the real problem women will have when they decide on any large scale to give up being angels will be the problem the individual woman has already found in the same decision. It is the immediate effect that this decision will have upon men. For a time women must expect from men a sort of collapse. What men have worked for will be gone. The little woman in the home, the wife whom it was the struggle of his life to shield from hardship and suffering of any kind, all those angels whose smooth faces and fur coats and diamond rings and well-kept mechanized homes were his prop and his pride and proofs of his success as man, will be removed. A real woman wants none of the false femininity of the angel about her. She likes work at least as well as the man does, she thrives on hardship, she enjoys a practical problem to be solved, she loathes the hours she has to spend keeping wrinkles out of her face, she despises having to waste time on the foibles of fashion. She wants to live and to enjoy herself and man and to feel her good brain working keenly and awarely in all she does. She is hearty and passionate and by nature an earth-loving creature when she gets the angel out of her system. She likes politics for the same reason man does, because it is an exciting and dirty game. She wants no privileges.

But man will have to be re-educated to the truth about women. He is used now only to angels. The idea of women instead of angels terrifies him. He at once begins to howl with Hitler that women ought to be locked into the home and kept pregnant as much of the time as possible. One of the most pitiful proofs of the weakness of any man as a man is when he begins that familiar yelp. It is a cry for protection. "For God's sake," he gasps, "get the women locked up!"

For men were weakened, too, when they made angels of their women. It is not the femaleness of woman that weakens and makes soft, but the femininity that man insists upon in the angel he wants to worship that ruins him. When will men be able to see their foolish inconsistency in adoring the "feminine" and not understand that this is the very femininity that they foster which is weakening themselves and the nation? The true female influence is hard and honest and realistic, as anyone knows who has observed a matriarchal society at work. There is nothing soft about it. Man has himself created the softness in our life by insisting on having angels around to worship and to worship him, to bolster his pride as a strong man, to provide solace at home for defeats outside, to make him sure of his doubtful strength.

Yes, if women decide to give up being angels, man is in for a hard and lonely time for a while. Who will tell him how wonderful he is, whatever he does? Who will subtly steal the smart out of defeat and make him feel sure of success next time? Who will keep his feelings from being hurt and maintain the fiction of his overwork and of his importance to the big boss, and his whole general indispensability? Nobody. It is going to be hard for him.

But women will have a still harder time for the same while. For it is, of course, inevitable that when women decide to stop being angels and just be ordinary human beings they will have on their hands a lot of unhappy, neurotic, terrified men, who will see nothing but the horror of a world run by women—or, let us say, a world not run solely by men. Men will be sulky, ferocious, and impossibly rude to women. "If women want it," they will say savagely, "let 'em have it!" And they will proceed to behave toward women as they would not dream of behaving not only to angels but even to other men. Women must expect this. And they will deserve it, some of the time, for, being inexperienced as human beings, they will make silly mistakes. They will be too bossy, for instance, because, having only men as their examples, they will think that bossiness is a proof of competence and superiority. And man will be properly infuriated, for he has so long been the boss. It is only natural that nothing makes a bossy man angrier than a bossy woman. Neither is to be blamed, but they will have to learn together that nobody needs to boss before happiness will come to them.

But before they can learn it there will be such a bad time that there will be individual women who will relapse into being angels out of sheer inability to go through with it. There may be many, for being angels for so long has weakened women's fiber, too. But real women will go through with what they must and bring patience and intelligence to work, and then there may come a day when men will find other things to spend their efforts upon that are better than fur coats and diamond rings for angels— world peace, for instance, and justice between races, and the economic stabilization of nations. And then he may find that he can dream greater dreams than he has ever dreamed before, and in true romance discover at his side, working with him, not an angel but a woman.

. . . Did I write it down a little while ago that women never dream? I was wrong. We do.

7. WOMEN AND WAR

WOMEN have for too long left men to struggle alone with the problem of evil in the world. And what is the problem of evil except the problem of wicked and ruthless individuals, the gangsters in a community, whether that community be a town, a nation, or a world? Protected by the walls of her home, busied in the peaceful pursuits of cooking and caring for children, woman has taken no responsibility for the control of wicked men, with the result that we see in the world today. In her security she has been too sentimental even to her own children. Women's sons stand at this very moment behind the machines of aggressive war and kill millions of innocent people. Women's sons are murdering and looting on a scale never before known in history. Is this not colossal proof of the failure of women to create moral character in her sons while they are in the home? If woman cannot create moral character in her sons while they are in the home, then she must help man to control evil character outside. For clearly it is beyond man alone to cope with evil, now that the will to evil of even a single man can be so magnified by modern weapons of war.

If we are ever to have peace, it will be accomplished not

by vaguely organized individuals passing resolutions. It will be accomplished only by bitterly determined men and women who will study and use every means in their power to enforce and indoctrinate the ideas and performance of peace. But the first step toward peace as the foundation of human relations will be a complete knowledge of what war is. We shall all have the knowledge of how war works when it breaks and what its effects are—that will be enforced upon us. But we need to know how it begins and who begins it and where and when.

War is, of course, endemic as yet in human society; and, like all endemic diseases, given certain conditions, it becomes epidemic at regular or perhaps irregular intervals. Those conditions are, if one reads the history of wars, two: first, discontent in a human group, that discontent being in the main economic; and, second, the rise to power of a certain type of mind. That type of mind is endemic, too. It is atavistic, cruel, simple, or cunning. But whatever it is, it is basically uncivilized. Thousands of years hence, unless such minds have destroyed us all, the creatures of a wiser age than ours will look back and recognize them for what they are—the persistent traces of our beginnings in the animal world from which we have so newly sprung. We are not free yet of the wild; the love of blood and the kill is still in us. Here is our true enemy, the enemy of us all, whatever our race and nation. These atavistic minds, hostile to kindness, resentful of slights which anyone must accept in life, remembering even the mishaps of childhood, resort to violence inevitably as their means of vengeance. We are too soft toward them. We are too apt to forgive them, saying, "Ah, if their childhoods had been better, they would have been better."

There is no proof of this. On the contrary, many of the best, the kindest, the most civilized and humane of men and women have suffered cruelly in childhood. But they were better for such suffering. They forgot it as they pressed on, or remembered it only to see that others were spared what they had suffered. They did not want to make all the world suffer because they once suffered, or dispel their youthful frustrations by machines of war crushing the bodies of the innocent and unknown. The suspicious jealousies of an ignorant tyrant who kills his intellectual superiors is an evidence not of an unhappy childhood, but of an atavistic and undeveloped mind; and, however shrewd and cunning and clever that mind may be, it is undeveloped if it proceeds against human society in tyranny and war. Let us not deceive ourselves. We have rightly discarded the old idea of Original Sin. And yet there is a truth in it. We are sprung from dark and earthy sources, and the mud clings to us yet in these atavistic minds who resort to animal force to gain their ends, an animal force heightened a million times when it extends itself through machines of war and death. These are dangerous minds, born dangerous first through confluences of blood and heredity we do not understand, made more dangerous by certain environmental conditions, and reaching their final climax when they are able, through finding at certain times, as they do, an environment suitable to them and an economic situation which they can exploit. War is the inevitable result of this meeting of the atavistic individual and the environment of general surrounding discontent.

What are we to do with such minds? Discern them, watch them, and bar at every step their rise to power. Let them function as individuals in a democracy, and never as officials or demagogues. How discover them? As children in school, as youths in college, as men in life. There should be psychiatrists' reports on them, and heed should be given the reports. We were all shocked a few years ago by a peculiarly brutal and it seemed aimless murder committed by a young man of some genius. That murder could have been prevented if a psychologist's report made upon him years before had been kept in mind. "This child," the report read, "will one day resort to violence." He did.

The minds which lead us to war are few. It would not be difficult to stop their rise to power. But it takes a method, a watchfulness, an energy for action which only determination for peace can provide.

To discover and to watch and to prevent the rise to power, therefore, of the atavistic individual is the first necessity for peace. Genghis Khan, Napoleon, Hitler—the mind is the same. It is as uniform as the symptoms of a known disease. It can be recognized, it can be prevented, and half of the basic cause for war eliminated.

The other half of the basic cause for war has to do with economic adjustments in a nation and between nations. Population pressures, unequal treaties, unjust tariff, the unfairnesses of trade, deprivation of raw materials, make national and international discontents which provide breeding places for war. There is full information on such places in newspapers, magazines, books. Foundations make constant research into such conditions. But nobody uses the information with the aim of discovering possible sources for war. We need as clear, as cold, as sacrificial a spirit for this as doctors have when they determine to eliminate a source spot of yellow fever or Asiatic cholera which threatens the world. War is the most devastating endemic and epidemic disease the human race has to endure, and yet too little has been done to discover and eliminate its cause by intelligent early control.

There must be a reason for this delay. It is to be found, I believe, in the mistaken estimate which men have made and still make of war when they do not see it as the inescapable result of certain knowable and removable causes. It is not possible to prevent war when all the causes which produce it have been allowed to flourish. But the causes can be prevented. That they are not prevented, that war is still accepted as a possible fate and destiny, even a glorious one, is the false notion which men still hold. The habit of men's minds is toward war. It may be that men alone can never make an end to war.

But women do not share the glories and pleasures of war. They are the ones who are left behind. They do not have the joy of comradeships, the excitement of adventure, the possible glory of victory or death. None of the glamour of war is theirs. They remain at home alone, that for which they lived gone. They take up the drab work in factories and fields which men have left. And when the men do not return, theirs is the burden of the postwar world. If the men do come back, nothing is the same, for no man goes through a war without being deeply wounded in spirit. Women have no illusions, or should have none, about what war is.

I believe that it is women who must end war if it is ever to be ended. It is women who must determine, by whatever ways of reason and deep emotion that they can use, that they will not go on having their work of bearing and rearing wasted by war or even the fear of war. Such determination is the first step. With it anything can be accomplished. Without it, we shall go on endlessly, generation after generation, with the sort of thing which faces us today.

To end war by the discovery and elimination of its individual and economic causes—here is a task great enough, human enough, useful enough to invite all women.

Hard? Yes, but not as hard as war!

Difficult to organize women? But not more difficult than to organize for war.

An international task? Yes, but do not imagine women anywhere like war any better than we do.

A complex job? Yes, but not more complex than war.

It would bring women into national and international affairs? Why not? She is able.

A long and slow job? Yes, but how endlessly long and slow war is, when its effects are felt generation after generation!

And what aim more suited to woman's creative nature than the bringing about of peace through the control of the two chief causes of war, the maladjusted individual and the depressed social group? Here is a field in which woman would have no competition with man, through which she could penetrate into thorough understanding of human problems, by means of which she could, if she would, influence government, by active participation or by group pressure. It is said too often that women have made no notable contribution to humanity except to bear children. Yet to continue to bear children only to have them slaughtered is folly. But to take as a solemn task the prevention of war would be an achievement unmatched. In the process women would become inevitably concerned in human welfare, to the betterment of all society as well as of themselves. It is the only hope I see of the end of war.

And it would give woman a job in the world. Actually women are becoming less and less necessary to the running of the world. It takes no great wisdom to see that woman is increasingly on the periphery of management. She was once the center of it. But those were the days when the center of civilization was the home, and she was the center of the home. Those were her days of power. In the whirl of centrifugal motion which is the movement of the human race the center of civilization has changed. Rather, it is changing. Where it will pause none knows yet, but it is now veering in the direction of the state. It will not end there finally, for it is in ceaseless motion. In history that center of civilization has been in many places. For long it was in the church, for long it was in universities. In pioneer countries it was always in the home. In periods of great industrial development it was in industry. In periods of expansion the center of civilization passed even into exploring. This is the political age, and human thought is centered in the ideologies of governments and in the organization for power, and never has woman been so remote from the vital growing centers of life as she is now.

For she is still struggling with the old, old question of whether or not she should stay in the home, without perceiving that the home as the center of life is already gone. Its roof is there and its four walls. Her beloved bric-a-brac is there, and the utensils for eating and sleeping and listening to the radio, which are the few necessities of life today. Yet even the necessities of life do not center in the home any more. Eating can be done anywhere at little cost and no trouble, and hotel beds are clean and comfortable and maybe less expensive than one's own. The truth, dreadful to women, is that the home is more and more of a luxury these days and less and less of a necessity except as a place to put women to keep them out of the way. Unless it can be brought back in some more necessary way, some day men are going to find that it is cheaper just to keep women in cells and cages or barracks or harems whence they can be summoned when service is wanted or the state needs new recruits. Women have always been relegated whenever men have relapsed into thinking that the sole important

functions of women are to service men and to breed children. Those are the times when the nonessentialness of
women is evident on every hand.

I have had a cold foreboding since the day I heard an
important executive in New York fume against the ap-
pointment of a woman to a government post in Washington. "But we'll soon change all that," he exclaimed. "We
don't want any women cluttering up things in Washington now."

In other words, when action is required women must be
got out of the way because they have no part in the vital
and actual work of the nation. All that they do can be dis-
pensed with in strenuous times except breeding and possibly caring for the sick and wounded. They enter industry,
it is true, in menial ways when men are called out of it for
war, but when men return they must again withdraw. In
the days of highly mechanized industry which are inevitably ahead of us there will be no use for women at all.
More than ever in that future women will have to knit,
and not only knit but unravel and knit again, just to have
something to do. The managerial age is approaching, and
unless woman can somehow educate herself to take her
share in the management of the world she will be relegated entirely. She is very nearly relegated now.

I do not feel disposed to blame men for this state of
affairs. I should be glad to hate them, for that would be
the simplest way of fixing blame. The simplest way of
starting a reform for women always is to begin by an attack upon men. Actually, the fault, if there is a fault, lies

in women themselves. The fault does not in every country lie with women. Obviously one cannot expect the Japanese woman, for example, oppressed by centuries of chatteldom, to take her place now by man's side, especially when the last thing a Japanese man wants is a woman at his side instead of under his feet. The recent announcement in Japan that women are to be kept out of all public office since their place is in the home is merely a laughable imitation of Japan's big brother for the hour, Germany. Japanese women never have come out of the home. It is significant, however, that no such announcement has come from China, and certainly in our country woman has had a good chance to take her place by man's side. Many men have waited for her to take it. She has had the liberty to do so.

But hers has been the fatal weakness of hesitation. Hesitating upon the threshhold of her home, uncertain whether to stay in or come out, she has tried to make her individual decision, not upon the basis of woman's worth or ability, but upon what man wants or would like. She has doubted the strength of her femaleness. She has been afraid of losing her femininity. And she has feared, if she lost it, that she would have nothing left wherewith to hold man's heart or attention. Instead of going boldly forth to join him, confident of the eternal female strength in her, sure of her own undying power to attract him when she wished to do so, she has settled back into her home and shut the door and waited, how often in vain, for him to come to her. Or she has sallied forth in shamefaced fashion, apologetically, as though she, too, thought she belonged at home, or she has come forth with hostility and hardness, and those are ugly traits.

The truth is that if a woman is a real woman and proud to be one, nothing can quench the essential femininity of her being. She may sit upon a throne and rule a nation, she may sit upon the bench and be a judge, she may be the foreman in a mill, she could if she would be a bridge builder or a machinist or anything else; and if she were proud of herself as a woman her work would be well done and her femininity deepened. It is when women undervalue themselves as women that they ape men and become mannish and arouse dislike in all their fellows, men and women. No kind of work can spoil the quality of a woman unless she has first spoiled it herself by wishing consciously or unconsciously that she were not a woman. This undervaluation of herself has made woman uncertain when she leaves the security of the familiar environment of home, and in her uncertainty she has too often imitated man, whom she fears, and she alternates in her behavior between repulsive mannishness and an apologetic, over-exaggerated, false femininity that is equally repulsive.

For the real female quality is something tough and strong and resistant. Women are not weak, except when they are uncertain of themselves. Once they are certain, they are whirlwinds of power and wells of strength. If they could have some sort of certainty that their femaleness was natural and right and ought not to be changed or quenched, they could and would take their places willingly by man's side. But they have for so long heard their qualities derided, they have for so long been called the weaker sex, they have for so many generations been told that they have no head for business and no understanding of government, that it would be more than human to expect them to have resisted the subtle degeneration of self-doubt.

The one good that men have conceded to women is moral superiority. Men have, or have pretended that they have, always expected women to be morally superior to them. So now, when a few independent women have gone out into business and government and have made use of the financial and legal and political tricks which men employ as a matter of course, there has been loud indignation that women are as dirty in business and politics as men are.

"What's the use of having women in politics," these furious males inquire, "if they are as bad as men?"

What use, indeed, are bad women anywhere, or bad men, or liars, male or female, or thieves or robbers or murderers, men or women? And what of the possibilities of good women, if woman were working at man's side, or are good women too troublesome outside the home?

This moral superiority which men have so generously given to women is as a matter of fact a very degenerating influence upon women. For, having no other superiority allowed her by man, she snatches at this poor rag of righteousness which he throws her out of the abundance of his strength and power over her, and she tries to make it cover her nakedness. If man had wanted to keep moral superiority, too, of course he would have done so. But he found it inconvenient in everyday life. To be as white as snow is not practical in business. Every little spot shows. It was a man cook I once had in China who conducted an earnest campaign in my house for several years to persuade and finally to force me to yield in the matter of dish towels of black instead of white linen. It would, he said, spare us both—me the trouble of incessant worry over dirty towels, and him the trouble of washing them every day. We parted at last, he male and I female to the end, on this matter of purity even in so utilitarian a matter as dish towels.

So have men always parted from women on practical righteousness. There is much to be said for men. Obviously it was easier for women to be good than men when women were shut up at home away from temptation to any of the major sins. If they developed the minor ones of laziness and pettiness and indifference and small lies and gossip, these became feminine weakness and did not greatly interfere with the bolder outlines of chastity and— I find I cannot think of another virtue for women, so let it go at chastity.

But why should men be astonished when woman coming forth at his side seems to be much the same stuff as he? The wonder is that she is not worse than he, because her righteousness is, after all, a hothouse thing, untried and untempted; and she has no real strength of her own to resist. She has not even his strength of experience to help her. He at least has sinned often enough to know the folly of sinning beyond a certain point. But she has had so little experience of sin that she cannot be blamed for folly or failing.

Besides, her righteousness, so long imposed upon her, has had very little reward. All the real rewards of goodness man has still kept for himself. Thus, though she is the angel, he is the priest, the prince of the church. It is he who addresses God, not she. She, poor thing, though so good that even he says she is better than himself, must sit in the pews and listen while he preaches, and she must bow her head when he prays to God on her behalf, and she must put in her bits of money when he passes the contribution box. I have always thought women got small reward from the church for all this righteousness of theirs. It does seem as though at least in the church, where moral worth is supposed to be required for entrance, woman ought to have some power. But no, man even devised a means of escape there. Though he demanded righteousness of woman he invented a religion which excused him from it. Righteousness was after all but filthy rags if one trusted to the blood of Christ for salvation, he proclaimed. The forgiveness of sins was made the great mercy of God, so that in a sense the greater sinner a man was, the more glory to God for washing him clean and accepting him as spotless. Thus did man make superiority out of his inferiority.

But practically he demanded righteousness of women, because it is inconvenient for a man to have an unrighteous wife. For one thing, if she is unrighteous he cannot be sure that he is the father of his sons, and there is fury and inconvenience in this. An unrighteous wife may bring trouble of all sorts in the home, and man cannot have trouble when he comes home at night. Indeed, women have had so little practical benefit from their superior righteousness that the sensible woman ought to discard righteousness altogether and take man's standards for her own. This would put men and women on an equal basis of moral worth and would do them both good. Men would see women as they are, and women could be rid of the degenerating effect upon them of a false valuation which they have taken far too seriously.

For, incredible as it may seem to the rational mind, many women do really believe that merely because they are women they are more moral than men—"nicer," if you like, more fastidious and purer and more spiritual. I cannot pronounce that word "spiritual" aloud. I have not done so in years. It arouses such feelings of repulsion and ferocity in me that I feel my tranquillity menaced. For, content with their so-called spiritual superiority, women have let their souls rot into pettiness and idleness and vacuity and general indifference in a world crying and dying for want of real superiority of spirit and moral worth, so that the spectacle does not bear contemplation. If women were really superior to men in righteousness or spirituality, could they sit blind and deaf and dumb, knitting their interminable knitting, crocheting and talking and going to teas and bridge parties and knitting

again, and filling the theaters day in and day out, and
rolling bandages and knitting again, and exchanging rec-
ipes and knitting, and re-arranging their furniture and
curling their hair and painting their nails and going to
style shows and knitting, knitting, knitting, while the
world goes down to darkness and dismay through lack of
bold goodness and moral integrity and real unselfishness?
Where is this moral superiority that will do nothing but
knit while heads roll off in revolutions and war crashes
upon our great cities so that ruins are all that we shall
have left if the world goes on as it now is?

Women have no moral superiority to man so long as
she will not come out of her selfish retreat and by man's
side work out with him the sort of democratic organization that the world must have if we are to live. We shall
have no change for the better until she does. We shall have
only increasing chaos and trouble as new wars release new
weapons upon us. For man has gone as far as he can without woman. The constant repetition in our life proves it.
Man by himself has not been able to make war obsolete,
as it should be among civilized people. Habituated to war,
conditioned to it as an inevitability, trained to consider it
as opportunity for his highest heroisms, man can scarcely
be expected to look cold-bloodedly at what has for so long
been his best chance for excitement, freedom, and glory.
The Nazi belief in the catharsis of war for men may be
partly true. It is a human necessity to find a certain release of self in sacrifice of self. Anyone is happier who does
not live for himself alone.

This loss of self is easier for woman than for man. However complex and selfish a woman is as an individual, when she has a child she goes down into a simple and elemental experience which drives self away, which divides that self into another and brings all of life into its simplest primeval terms. There never was a woman who was not the better for it, however inadequate she may be afterwards in nurturing and training her child. Women are cleansed in soul by this return to the elements of death and life that make childbirth, and any woman who has not had the experience is and feels incomplete. Sublimation there may be, but she searches for it, aware of her incompleteness.

But in our changed world man has no such opportunity left him any more for return to the elemental. Once he had it, perhaps, in the hunt, the chase, the risk of death. For the loss of self carries with it always the risk of death, and death has a fearful and endless charm for the human creature. It is as though in the dark places of his being there hides always the awareness of his end, and that awareness leads him, as moth to candle, to approach death again and again. The risk of death in childbirth exalts the woman. She goes down to the gates of death and she comes back triumphant over death. But man has no equivalent of this experience, and his being craves it and he devises it out of war. Generation after generation he devises it in one way and another, and as it approaches he dreads and fears it, and when it is come he welcomes it and exalts himself through it.

For war to man, like childbirth to woman, is simplifying in its emotions and activities. All the real problems of life can be put aside while the one thing is done and little thought is needed to do it. He gives himself up to the familiar process. There is for him an actual relief in having an expected war break. His hatreds can be expressed without censure, he can let his emotions run free, he can behave as dramatically, as heroically as he likes, and no one laughs at him. It is almost impossible for a man to behave heroically in the cool and ordinary times of peace. But in war anything is allowed him, he is praised and applauded and made much of, as women are excused and allowed for in pregnancy. It is inevitable then, in a world controlled by men without women, that we shall have wars and disorders recurrent. Only when women take their full share in the directing of history can there be a balance which will then do away with such disturbances.

What can be offered to man as a substitute for the blood bath of war? Where shall he go for glory? That question man must answer for himself. The skies are open to him with all their stars and suns, the earth is beneath him full of materials he does not know. The very air in which he moves is waiting with its secrets for him to plumb. How necessary is the blood bath for men and women? Civilized women by the million these days must do without the elemental experience of childbirth. Only a return to polygamy could give children to all women. It may be not too much to ask that civilized man do without war.

But war, of course, carries to men sweets beyond itself.

War automatically puts men in places of power. All men who wish women to retreat, love war, for war helps them. Every war sets women back a generation, and this in spite of industrial gains for them. For those gains are in small places, and women have to give a good share of them up again when the men come home. They would be called ungrateful if they did not; and, besides, they may as well, for laws would be devised to compel them. Psychologically and emotionally, war sets women back both in man's mind and in their own. For man comes home from war a spoiled creature, and one too often weakened by self-pity and conceit. He has had to be pampered and praised into considering himself a hero so that he would be a hero, and everyday life is flat after war, and his wife must go on with the pampering and praising or he will feel her unappreciative. It is for him amazingly like childbirth for the woman. She behaves like that after she has successfully had a baby.

Men and women will have to work out some sort of compromise on this matter of having wars and babies. They manage to negate each other as it is. Women fulfill themselves in having the babies, and men fulfill themselves in destroying them. There ought to be some other more profitable form of pleasurable sacrifice for the human race than this sacrifice of the innocents.

8. THE EDUCATION OF MEN
AND WOMEN
FOR EACH OTHER

EQUALITY, of course, is no easy matter except for talk. Only careful education can make people equal. There is no equality in indivduals, that we know. But how can man be persuaded that woman is his equal until he is educated in that knowledge, and how can woman be persuaded that she can and ought to be man's equal except by education in that knowledge?

It is perhaps timely at this moment for men and women to consider this question of their basic relationship to each other, since the actual danger of fascism inevitably is that, in one way or another, with or without war, all the world will be affected by it. Brain touches brain, and emotion stirs emotion; and even in a determined democracy we shall not escape some infusion of fascism. That infusion will run and spread in the channels of traditionalism, and we Americans are nowhere so traditional as in the relationship between men and women.

My own anxieties about fascism have less to do with women than with men. For when woman goes back to medievalism she never goes back alone. She always takes man back with her. In proportion as she becomes a slave, he becomes a slave owner, and of the two the slave is the less harmed. Slaves develop great qualities of character, endurance, philosophy, diplomacy, humor, secret strength of resistance, and the ability to keep their own counsel even to the point of slyness. Out of all this they learn to rule, and they gain, if they have any wits, the real ascendancy over their masters.

Thus the consequences of fascism for men are very serious, and the more serious because there are so many American women who look with longing at the comfortable restrictions of fascism which would take beyond woman's power of decision the difficult question of whether or not her place is in the home. For women have long had to be devious creatures, as we all know, and many a woman would welcome the possibilities for power which slavery gives her, and secretly many a woman would enjoy the power joined with total lack of responsibility which a slave has. A slave need not worry about improvements in society or in the community. She can leave all that to her owner, man. She need not worry even about her food and drink, her clothing, or the roof over her head. These are provided to slaves as a matter of course. She has her little labors well defined each day, but there are no laws for slaves to compel them to speed or to standards of production; and, above all, in slavery woman has entire mental leisure. The world is not her affair. She can devote all her powers to thinking up new means to have her own way and so to become man's ruler.

I am alarmed for American men in this approaching wave of fascism because they have been so foolish as to grant all the privileges of freedom and democracy to women without compelling them to share any of the practical responsibilities in return. Here society requires no real service from women, though it extends to them in fullest measure its advantages and protection, even to the point of giving them education. All this ought to terrify any thinking man, for when the wave of fascism hits him and he succumbs to it, probably unaware for the moment that he has done so, he will have in the nursery, the kitchen, the church, no ignorant peasantlike creature sharpening her few wits as best she can, but a clever, subtle being whose development, body and mind, has long been the equal of his own and whose energies are often superior to his. I am glad I am not a man in America.

The truth is that under no form of government and in no civilization has the relationship between men and women been entirely satisfactory to man. One of woman's most hateful qualities has been that she can make the best of anything and somehow emerge to be an annoyance, and man suffers. I have never seen a country, and I have seen many, where man was not in some way or another annoyed by woman, by her inferiority and by her superiority. The one possible solution for the problem of woman has never been tried. It is simple equality with man. This seems never to have occurred to him.

I was forcibly reminded of this a while ago when I was being called upon by the benevolent middle-aged president of a midwestern college for women, who came to ask help in educating his "girls." He said, looking the picture of innocent manhood:

"It is my aim to educate women to be the partners of men."

I could not repress a groan. Here was the same old notion of inequality.

"But who," I inquired, "is educating men to be the partners of women?" For, I thought, how can men and women be partners if they are not being educated for each other?

We parted irrevocably upon that, for he could not see what I meant and I could not blame him. The education of men and women for real equality with each other has now become extremely difficult, not only to perform but even to think about, because of their long education away from each other. And yet in this strange pause before the tidal wave of fascism hits us, I recommend men to take thought of what may befall them under that wave and to consider how to force women to equality with them— equality of responsibility, equality of knowledge—lest they assume again man's old yoke of subservience to a creature ignorant and selfish and fundamentally irresponsible to anyone but herself.

I use the word "forcibly" with purpose, for I repeat that I discern in an alarming number of women a yearning for the fleshpots of slavery. Nothing has brought this more clearly home to me than a certain poll taken some months ago among the students of a woman's college, ironically enough an institution founded by a woman for the education of women. Those students put themselves on record as overwhelmingly against any woman's being considered as eligible for the presidency of the United States, the vice-presidency, or even the office of Cabinet member. Their reasons for this return to medievalism are even more amazing than the act itself. They said with apparently calm self-abasement that women lack the necessary physical and emotional stability; that women have not sufficient experience in public affairs; and that women cannot "escape the pettiness of life."

The only reason I can guess for this extraordinary document is the venom that women seem to have for women in the competition in a society where there is neither freedom nor the fixed pattern of traditions between men and women. I have not yet found a satisfactory explanation for it. The only possible one is that in a free society such as ours where women may do as they like if they have the courage to change old traditions, they have only themselves or each other to blame if they fall short of their potentialities; and, being human, they will scarcely blame themselves. In Japan, for instance, women are quite tenderly loyal to one another; for there, as in the newer fascist countries, women have been given limits beyond which they may not go. Thus none need envy another's irritating progress. All must stop at the same point. Women's jealousy of women there is of the small and harmless sort found between two women contending for the same man in a household. It does not reach out, as it does here, in such large prejudices as affect government, industry, and learning, illustrated in such ways as the unwillingness that women show in seeking professional services from women, and in the hostility they show instinctively toward any woman above the average in achievement. Indeed, it would not be surprising if women here would prefer never to have a woman president of this country merely because she was a woman, or perhaps because only one of their number could sit in that seat of honor and responsibility. In the Orient poison would be the weapon used or a dagger in the dark under the left breast of a sleeper.

It will take a good deal of wisdom on the part of man to realize his danger as fascism approaches him, and after he knows it will take even more self-control not to give way, as German men have, to his natural inclination to lock women up. The American man will be especially tempted because he does not like women nearly as well as, for example, the Chinese man or the Frenchman does. He has already suffered too much from them through his ignorance of them; and, moreover, his sense of humor is not so sophisticated as that of the French and Chinese. What he must somehow bring himself to remember is that if he locks women up he is going to suffer more and in far more important ways than he does now. He is going to be undermined as the Chinese man has been undermined, and as has the Frenchman. If he realizes his danger and keeps woman free, of course he must still not think of liberty and equality as the rope with which woman will hang herself, for she will not hang herself in any case. She

161

is too smart for that. But only through liberty and equality will woman be forced to share man's responsibility in the world so that she can no longer enjoy the easy and irresponsible life of the slave, and only then perhaps can there be hope that after sufficient education man and woman can begin to live as they ought to live, with the burden of life divided between them fairly to the benefit of both.

Perhaps then man will like woman, for she will be likable as she never has been, and when woman feels that man likes her, her present discontent will be gone completely and permanently. For woman feels the dislike of man as she feels nothing on earth, and it shakes her to the very core of her being. She is made utterly insecure by it, and no other security can make her feel safe because when man dislikes her she has no confidence in herself, and because she has no confidence in herself every woman enters into a tremendous rivalry, though she may not know it, with every other woman. Thus she is pleased and delighted when her lover tells her, as every man does tell some one woman, that she is not like any woman on earth. For a while she hopes and believes this is true. It is a very brief while, and few there be who can delay its end, and sweet though it is to the man it is sweeter to the woman. Sooner or later he perceives that she is after all only a woman, and the cloud of his dislike of woman begins to temper and to shadow even his love, and she is desolate or cynical according to her temperament.

There are, of course, innumerable mild-mannered American men and gentlemen who will protest that they have never disliked women—on the contrary, and so forth. It is platitudinous to reply that one often harbors a feeling without being aware of it. It is only just to agree that there are exceptions. But if there could be a poll delicate enough to measure the things people will not tell, the mass of men's dislike for women would mount much higher than their liking.

I am constrained to this conviction as an observer by mere evidence piled on evidence, by the frank private conversations of men with each other when they "always except those present," by executives who complain of the women in their employ for faults in women which are not noticed in men or seem less considerable in men, by husbands who find their real pleasure and relaxation away from their wives rather than with them, by sons who sentimentally adore their mothers to the point of hatred and who obey them through fear without healthy rebellion, by the general and far from tacit opposition to women's rising to any place of important executive power in business or other organizations, by the usual practice of giving a woman employee less money for the same work a man might do, by boys who believe themselves better than their sisters and all girls, and who grow up into men who think themselves better than their wives and all women merely because their physical shape is not quite the same, by the common jokes of a people which always betray them. We laugh at exaggerations of the truth, but there must be truth or we do not laugh. And there are too many jokes made upon the subject of the naïveté and folly of women in America for me to discount their meaning and significance. But time fails to tell of all evidences of man's dislike for woman. They are here for all to see who will use impartial eyes.

There is a basis for this dislike, of course. Psychologists have already given us one very sound one. As society is organized in the United States, our children, boys and girls alike, receive almost all of their early discipline from women, and to the child discipline means refusal. Those first refusals are very important, for they are never forgotten. The memory of those first no's, great and absolute, sticks in the subconscious. And the American mother says most of them because the American father is not at home much. Then a woman schoolteacher says them because American men consider primary-school teaching beneath them, though this is true in no other country to any such extent. American boys and girls have to reach high school before they associate discipline with men.

And woman has another disadvantage. Man comes to her too much as a suppliant, and a suppliant he remains too long, and it adds to his dislike of her that this is so. If he forces her against her will, she who thus accedes has subtle and fearful weapons of revenge, and the more sensitive the man the more he is wounded by her. Whether he is aware of it or not, his earliest life is shaped by a woman, and the core of his happiness, his poise, his satisfaction with himself and with all else in life, if it does not actually depend upon a woman, is so entwined, or so entangled with her, that to a degree he is helpless without

164

her and helpless with her, and so what can he do but hate her for this? The more illogical, the more unreasonable, the more ignorant and foolish and incompetent she is, the more he hates her because she is a power over his memory and his life. The individual woman who has him at her mercy for the moment becomes for him a symbol of all women. For only in the brief hour of romantic love is the average man convinced that one woman is essentially different from the others. The rest of his life he enjoys a grim or gay compensatory humor at her expense, and it pleases him to repeat that it is just like a woman to be—whatever he thinks she is, a gad-about, a time-waster, an incompetent, a cat, a nagger, a whore, or a dangerous and unreliable automobile driver.

And yet when she is none of those things, when she is brilliant and able and competent, he dislikes her in a more subtle fashion because then he is afraid of her, and fear is added to the power of those childhood shapes.

Such is the situation between American men and women, summarized. It assumes new acuteness in view of the great changes which fascism forces upon the relationship of men and women anywhere. It has already been so augmented by traditions of Western chivalry, which have imposed false standards of sex upon men and women alike, that in spite of new acuteness one is tempted to leave it alone. After all, the lover of *laissez faire* may say, the primary requirement for the sexes is the production of children, and nature cunningly compels men and women to this whether they like each other or not.

Unfortunately human beings seem to require something more than physical reproduction of themselves for their happiness and well being. Procreation occupies too little space in the normal span. There are years before it begins and after it is over. And, besides, at no time in her life is any woman not feeble-minded content with merely having children; and under a monogamous system such as ours man deserves more satisfaction than the physical even with one woman. In polygamous society it is true that a man, if he is so inclined, may keep himself fairly occupied in the simple repetitive ways of physical sex provided he is not too intelligent and asks for nothing beyond. But if he is intelligent even then the repetition palls. I have known polygamists of subtle taste and intelligence who actually found their real excitement in discovering women with whom they had no physical relations whatever, who found their keenest satisfaction in the varied exchange of ideas and feelings, an exchange permeated as they made it with the essence of sex. But I must confess that the men as well as the women in these cases were unusual, as all artists are unusual, and so should be passed over in any general discussion of men and women. And yet my memory returns to them because of the extraordinary pleasure they found in each other as men and women.

For the unfortunate result of the present relationship between American men and women is that, since they do not much enjoy each other, both are missing the core of life—the zest, the sharpness, the contrast, the gaiety which

mutual appreciation and understanding between two differing persons gives them both. Reforms cease to press
upon those who are gay and well content, and how many
crises would never come about if men and women were
educated to appreciate and understand each other can be
imagined merely by reading the daily newspapers.

The question still to be answered, however, in this
search for the satisfying relationship between men and
women is, does woman need to be educated? Fascism of
the German type and certain of the Oriental civilizations
say not. We in our own country have never been much
influenced by others, and need not be now were it not for
the ripplings of the wave of fascist thinking already to be
found here and inevitably to increase as war atmosphere
increases, even though it be only defense preparation for
war. The question may therefore answer itself in our
country. In spite of the willingness of many women to retreat from the responsibilities of full equality in citizen-
ship with men, most American women have perhaps been
given too much liberty to enable them again to be slaves.
It is easy to set slaves free, and there is also the pleasure
of having performed an act of righteousness. But to make
slaves of the free-born, how difficult that is and what
specious reasoning must be invented and enlarged upon
to provide the sense of justification so necessary to a moral
people like ourselves! It would be revolting to American
men, too, to think of restricting and enslaving a group to
which their mothers belong. Even though they might not
object to a *fait accompli* if it could be accomplished with-

out their being responsible for such ungallantry, their dislike for women as a whole is nearly always tempered with sentimental regard for some "little woman."

And there is that other unfortunate result which they could not hope to escape: that women, when they are kept ignorant and enclosed, relapse into superstition and primitiveness, and inevitably they infuse into their sons the attitudes of mind natural to such states. No later education, as anyone knows who is familiar with people who keep their women socially and politically subordinate to men, can undo this unfortunate result of early years when for physical reasons even male children must stay for a time with their mothers. Men never recover from the ignorance of their mothers. It is true in the profoundest sense that the progress of a people is in direct proportion to the development of its women as human beings. Here may be the Achilles heel even of fascism.

It seems scarcely practicable, therefore, unless women themselves insist upon it, to force American women to return exclusively to the nursery, the kitchen, and the church. Even those lazy women who would like the return might refuse if they realized how many of their privileges would be taken from them. Women in the nursery-kitchen-church sort of society cannot come and go as they like, or say what they please, or enter into a tenth of the pleasurable pastimes which American women take as a matter of course. Moreover, women would have to give at least lip service to the male who owns her and after all these years of speaking her mind that might be the most difficult part of the subjugation, both to exact and to endure.

American women have been, of course, in what is locally called "a soft spot." Nothing is expected of them except what they wish of their own will to undertake, they have no real responsibilities for the nation or to the nation, and they may come and go as they like. This sounds perfect and would be except for the fact that with it all women have not somehow won men's real liking or even their respect. Because of this one fact women lack everything, for without the liking and respect of men the life of women is tasteless to them. And out of woman's consequent discontent flow a multitude of evils.

What is the solution for our situation? Simply this—a new education, the education of men and women for each other. We need an education which would enlighten us about each other and would have as its object the removal of the separation between men and women by educating them as true equals. The emphasis by tradition upon our different functions as men and women has made and kept us separate. There has never been any real research into the much-talked-of necessity of differing functions in men and women. So far as we actually know the only exclusively male function is the begetting of children and the only exclusively female function is the conception of children, together with their birth and suckling. This is the sole premise for the education of men and women for each other. Beyond that all is surmise and the result of prejudice for reasons far from the facts.

Where should the education of men and women for each other begin? First, in the complete rejection of the idea that the two great and inevitable groups of human beings, male and female, should have their activities predetermined by the automatic criterion of sex. We inveigh against race prejudice and yet what we say to women is what we say to the Negro: "Because you are thus, you shall forever be barred from every activity except housework and the care of young children. If you enter the industries it shall only be in the lowest positions and at whatever pay you can get, regardless of what men are given for the same pay. If you enter the professions, you shall be continually held back from any important advancement." Profound as race prejudice is against the Negro American, it is not practically as far-reaching as the prejudice against women. For stripping away the sentimentality which makes Mother's Days and Best American Mother Contests, the truth is that women suffer all the effects of a minority.

There was once, of course, every reason why the activities of men and women should be sharply divided—the man to the outdoors, the woman to the indoors.

Has woman, then, no function left in the home? In comparison to what she once had, no, in a practical sense. Emotionally, yes, as much as ever. That is, she has the important work of giving to child and man the feeling of home and security where she is. She is still their center, though home is not. They must feed upon her as their source of comfort and upholding love. In the old days this was easy for her, for material activities gave her the means of expressing what she was to them. They depended upon her for bread and for love, and she made both together. But now love and comfort must be expressed through bakers' bread and refrigerated food, through garments bought at department stores, and bedtime stories on the radio. Words are all she has left of her own, and words are not enough for the full expression of the love she feels.

Her attempts to supply moral teaching, too, are obviously inadequate, as the state of the world now proves. Indeed, as a teacher of morals women must confess their failure. It takes a boy very little time after he leaves the home at six to realize that the world outside the home has standards very different from those his mother gives him. He soon learns to leave her teachings at the gate, and to live according to what he finds outside. Nor does he take the trouble to explain this to her. Perhaps he could not explain if he would, since the knowledge is instinctive and is learned so young. Explained or not, it goes with him through life, and has been known for centuries as the double standard. All that woman has gained from her endeavor to be man's moral teacher has been the lonely task of practicing what she preached. Man has expected her to do that, while he has considered her teachings impractical for himself.

And man is right in so far as he declares her teaching impractical. How can she teach him standards which she herself cannot test and try in the world where his life is? How dare women ask or expect of men codes of behavior perfectly possible only to women, shut into the isolated security of home but impossible perhaps to anyone in a man's world? Women can ask nothing, expect nothing, in moral improvement in the world unless they go out into that world and take their share in its work. Nor can they prepare their children morally for a world which they themselves do not know by actual sharing of its responsibilities.

Woman must follow into the world those activities which once were hers in the home. She must busy herself again with problems of food and housing and education and religion and government. Her task of creating an environment for her children she must go on doing in the community, in the nation, in the world, since home has ceased now to be the real environment for man and child. She must follow man and child and live where they live if she is to continue to be to them what once she was in the preservation of life and the stimulation of mind and spirit.

Until she does this, moreover, she cannot find in herself the springs which feed them. For woman has no supernatural qualities, no direct connection with heaven. She is a fumbling human creature, as easily inclined to discontents and peevishness as any other; and she cannot achieve character or nobility alone within four walls full of plumbing and electricity. She can only achieve it today as she used to achieve it, through work and equal responsibility with man. In those days she could and did speak with authority, for she knew what she was talking about.

Now it must be confessed she talks too often without knowing. Her functions and duties, in short, even though they remain the same, are no longer exclusively in the home. They are waiting, undone, in the nation and in the world. When she does them we shall know the difference.

But she will not do them in her present state of mind. That state of mind is, as I have said, uncertainty. That phrase, "Woman's place is in the home," exhausted as it is from repetition, nevertheless carries a significance beyond its literal meaning. For modern women who have no idea of remaining literally shut up in the home still take cover under the phrase. Though they go forth to office and to pleasure every day, they leave their minds behind them at home, tied up like little dogs to bedposts. They go forth, brightly vacuous, to tap typewriters, to sit in hairdressers' booths, to dawdle through department stores or to clerk there, or only to lie on sun-soaked beaches. But they leave their minds at home, and with no sense of any responsibility they come and go, seeing poverty and maladjustment everywhere and relating it never to themselves or to what they could do. Still, sometimes they do keep their hearts in their bodies and then in pity they undertake vast charities and good works. But what is really wanted is their minds, and these they keep at home. Minds, intelligent, determined minds, are what the world needs today; and women have them exactly as much as men do, if they would only bring them along when they go out from home.

173

Who can persuade them of this? No one, I think, except men. I have told how in China, when the anti-foot-binding reform was going on, it was women who refused to give up foot-binding. Mothers dared not take the risk of not binding their little daughters' feet, lest at sixteen and seventeen men might find them ugly and so unmarriageable. It was only when men themselves began to like girls with natural feet that the reform was real. Chinese men found it fun to have women at their sides in work and play instead of hobbling about courtyards. So American men might find it fun to have their women really at their sides in work as well as play if women had their minds with them. But until American men discover this, as the Chinese did, I fear women will not dare to bring their minds out of the home. Whether they should or not, women still shape themselves by what men like, at least until they have secured their goal of marriage.

The trouble with this idea of woman's shaping herself to man's wishes is that she can never quite do it, at least in America. She is not being educated for it. If man is to be the superior he wants to be, then everything ought to be shaped to a dictatorship of man—that is, women ought to be trained and taught only to be what man wants woman to be, and men ought to be trained to want only certain attainable things in women. Character, for instance, ought not to be expected. It is unreasonable to expect women to develop character without responsibility. It is impossible, in fact. Character remains pure theory unless there is opportunity to exercise it. Intelligence, too, if it is to develop, must be allowed scope. It atrophies when it is not used. This is why so many women have little character and less intelligence by the time they reach a certain age, however promising they were up to twenty-five. It is not because they are women that they have become effeminate, but because life has made too few demands on them. Men in like circumstances become as effeminate. If men want women to be different, they must demand it.

Do women want to be different from what they now are? Under their layers of vanity and childish sensitivity to anything which questions their perfection as angels, do they not? The American woman is so natively intelligent, so potentially able, so filled with fine energy, that it seems inevitable that she would like to feel herself used to the height of her capacity, as certainly she is not now. What is happiness if it is not the knowledge that all capacities are being fully used? And what is woman's tragedy except the knowledge that what she has she cannot give, what she is she cannot be?

Yet how can man know what he wants in woman when all that he can know is what he has had and that has too often irked and wearied even while it charmed him? Men and women are in an impasse as regards each other. And yet actually the trouble is the same. Each is bound by tradition, the tradition of woman in the home.

Tradition, then, is the culprit. But what can be done about tradition? Only one thing—break it. Being dead, it is always breakable. There is only one question—how to begin to make a new one. Obviously, intelligent people will have to begin, for the unintelligent always cling to old tradition for security. I suppose it is fair to say that the greatest concentration of intelligence is in our schools. At any rate, schools are as good a place as any to begin.

Let it be proposed, therefore, that, instead of men being educated solely for the industries, the professions, and the sciences, and women educated for nothing in particular, the primary aim of our schools and colleges should be to educate men and women for each other. There is nothing impractical or unreasonable in this; indeed, it is the only education that can be really education for life. Since harmony and understanding between men and women is the only basis for a tranquil and wise society, is it not folly deliberately to educate men and women away from each other, as we are now doing, actually if not consciously?

I can hear anxious teachers crying out, "But what would be the program for such a re-orientation of education?" A teacher without a program is helpless. But I am no expert in teaching and no believer in programs, and I will only suggest the foundations upon which such a program can be built.

First, men and women should go to school together from the day they start kindergarten to the last hour of the Ph.D. examinations. But they should not be graded, as they are now, according to their physical ages. They should be put together at their biologic ages when, male and female, they are closest together and most able to understand each other. A girl of six is the same biologic age as a boy of seven, and a girl of fifteen as a boy of seventeen or eighteen. When they are graded together as they now are, male and female, we work them harm. Who can tell how deep are the resentments which the boy feels against the girl, always apparently his superior in the school system? And there are those far deeper hostilities aroused when she in her fifteen-year-old urges presses her instinctive attentions upon the fifteen-year-old boy, biologically unready for her and therefore afraid of her and resentful of her frustration and repelled by her, and yet somehow degraded in his own eyes with mortification at his own inadequacy. Who can blame him if in later years he hastens to assert and to maintain his superiority, and who can blame her if she never wholly forgets his rebuffs and doubts forever the rightness of her own being? Biological age mating should begin with the kindergarten.

Second, from the first day to the last of formal schooling men and women should be taught exactly the same things by the same persons. The whole body of knowledge, including all techniques, should be taught in exactly the same way to men and to women. The knowledge of homemaking and child-care and all the realm of what has been mistakenly called women's work should be given to men and women together, for theirs together should be the responsibility in the home as well as outside it. It is the only way to bring the home back, to make it again the mutual work of man and woman together. For what made the pioneer home so valuable to man and woman was that their work was done there together. The new education of man and woman for each other should aim at the creation again of a home for the modern family which can fill its needs in these times as the pioneer home did for its time.

For it may be said and not altogether humorously, that our present unequal education has worked great hardship upon men. Many a man born to be a home-maker has been compelled by tradition to be something else. The injustice has been grave to women, too. No one will ever know what discoveries and creations have been suppressed because women who ought never to have gone near a kitchen were imprisoned there by the same tradition that forbade its delights to men. Such women should have had their children, but should never have cooked for them or cared for them. Their motherhood could have been far more valuably used in other ways both for the individual children and for society.

For until scientists can discover the trick of heredity that will insure men's being born with certain traits and women with others, we must still bear with the unfortunate fact that men and women inherit equally from their ancestors. The simple reason why women have not been as productive in the arts and sciences and professions as men have been is that they have not been allowed to be or encouraged to be, and the two are one. And the reason why so many homes are badly run and fussily managed is because the women who run them ought not to be there at all. Men with a genius for home management should be doing it. And yet few men and few women are endowed with sufficient courage to flout tradition and do what they ought and want to do as individuals.

All knowledge in common, then, and taught in exactly

the same way, should be the new education for men and women. Let there be no secrets between them, either of trade or sex. Roughly speaking, half of the curriculum should be devoted to trade knowledge, one quarter of it to study about women, and the other quarter to study about men, but all of it studied together under the same teachers.

All of that great body of knowledge which I have crowded into the word "trade" must be taught with a new emphasis. Heretofore it has been mistakenly assumed to belong to man. But with this new attitude in education of men and women for each other, this, of course, must be changed. This common education for and with each other ought to remove much if not all of the strain now found between men and women. If women know that they are given the technical equipment of knowledge which men have, they will have a sense of security and self-confidence. If they do not or cannot marry, they can take care of themselves. Similarly, a man, if he knows everything about home-making, need not be anxious about his ability to hold a technical job. He may find his place in some good woman's home, and with her work out the perfect partnership, unhampered and unshamed by the traditions of sex segregation.

But curriculum subjects in themselves will have to be revised. History, for example, has always been taught entirely as the work of man. When woman appears in it she is either as a queen of little practical use, or a rebel smashing up furniture with axes or praying in saloons. The truth has never been told about women in history:

that everywhere man has gone woman has gone too, and what he has done she has done also. Women are ignorant of their own past and ignorant of their own importance in that past. In curiosity a few months ago I asked a haphazard score of women of my acquaintance if they had ever heard of Elizabeth Cady Stanton. Only one had even heard her name, and she had no recollection of more. Yet only a generation ago Elizabeth Cady Stanton was called the greatest woman in the United States, and by some the greatest in the world. If women are as ignorant as this of themselves they can scarcely expect men to know more. But if the aim of education is to be the enlightening of men and women about each other, of course history must be taught truthfully about both, and truthfully rewritten.

Psychology, as another example, should be taught with definite consideration of mental differences between men and women, with thought given and research made over a space of time as to whether such differences are based upon physiology or environment, and whether they are permanent. There should be anxiety to prove nothing between men and women, but merely to discover the truth about each other. This new education of men and women for each other would remove the tedious rivalry which now poisons so much of the relationship between the sexes. Women need not be anxious to prove themselves superior to men, nor eager to prove all women inferior to men because they fear they themselves are inferior. And men need not be anxious to prove themselves superior to all women out of the fear that they are not. It will be taken for granted that such superiorities and inferiorities are to be found only in individuals and that no one is doomed by sex.

Psychology should embrace the whole important psychology of sex. We Americans are childishly interested in the least important aspects of sex because we are so ignorant. Nobody really teaches us anything about sex at home or in school. "Why are adults in your country so absorbed with sex?" is the frequent question of the foreign visitor to our land. The reply is obvious, "Because we know so little about it."

Yet our interest, out of our very ignorance, extends scarcely at all beyond the physical, and we are ignorant indeed of sex in its complex and fascinating and important aspects. If one asks the principal of a school what is being taught his pupils about sex, he speaks of its most elementary terms. The essentials of the physical relation between the sexes as a preparation for marriage is simple and easily taught. It is to be summed up in the one axiom that is vitally important, which is that of the discovery of the cycles of passion natural to the two individuals concerned and the mutual adjustment necessary between them. Anything beyond that grows out of such adjustment and may or may not be taught as further technique. It is true that we have much to discover about passion in the woman and passion in the man. I venture a guess that, male and female, they are fundamentally much more alike than they now seem. Man's apparent lack of rhythm might be changed to a rhythm as definite as woman's if he had full opportunities of companionship with her in all of life. As it is, the physical relation between men and women is burdened and made too urgent with their need for completer union in all ways.

But the whole delicate being of a man and the whole delicate being of a woman, how important that they be made known to each other, not only in terms of history and psychology, but through literature and especially through poetry and the novel! Why do men write more good plays than women do and stronger poetry, and why do women write the subtler novels and the lovelier verse, and what is music in the man and why has woman through the ages been so silent and who can free the music in her, since music there must be, God not having forbidden it to her? All of literature is an illumination of men and women in relation to each other and so it should be studied by them both together. For literature is not a thing in itself. It is not absolute. It is valuable only for what it reveals about men and women.

But it is idle to enumerate one curriculum subject after another even in their most general terms in relation to men and women. The aim of the whole teaching of boys and girls should be the removal of the present antagonism between men and women, an antagonism caused by the difference of emphasis, by fear and mutual distrust, and these caused by ignorance. Not the least benefit of this change would be in that part of their life where men and women must remain eternally separate because they are male and female, where sex antagonism is now too often inevitable because there is no sex friendship.

The result of this education for sex friendship would be the breaking down of the tradition which dooms woman to one sphere and man to another. Men and women should own the world as a mutual possession. As things are now they divide it into separate domains, and each strives to rule absolutely in his part, if not in the other's. When either enters the domain not his, he must subjugate himself or herself, and no one likes a lifetime of subjugation, especially when it is not accompanied by love or even by friendship. Men and women must be educated out of that wish for power in any domain; and they can be, for the root of any wish for power is to be found in insecurity of some sort and in distrust of others through ignorance of them. We do not want to rule those whom we trust and understand.

And when woman especially is educated mentally and spiritually beyond her little domain, as she has been in our country, without being given a share or taking a share for herself of a larger domain, her power becomes dangerously concentrated. She assumes, for instance, far too much responsibility for the children, who belong no more to her than to man; and this power extends over a far longer period than it should. She regulates too much and controls too long the lives of the children. Man allows this because tradition has given her this domain. Tradition is wrong, and men lose much through not sharing in the care and responsibility of children from their birth. But most of all the children are injured. I hear too many women say, "It takes all my time and thought to run my home and care for children." It does because woman is usurping the power in the home. She ought not to run the house and the children. What business is it of hers to assume control over something so mutual to a man and a woman as their home and children?

And yet man has been as ruthless in his own power over the domain outside. He has been responsible for the environment which surrounds children when they leave the doors of their homes, and that he has not made a very good job of it suggests that he might have done better had he insisted on woman's sharing that responsibility. His children have suffered through him because he has kept woman out of his domain except in small subordinate ways.

Let woman out of the home, let man into it, should be the aim of education. The home needs man, and the world outside needs woman. Children need their fathers at home and they need their mothers outside of it. That is, the work of the world needs to be done by men and women together. Who knows but that the influence of the man might solve the problems of the problem child, and who knows but that the practical and realistic brains of the woman might devise a way to discern and prevent early the causes of war? At least women know the long cost of giving birth to and training those children who as men can be killed in the fraction of a second. And men might realize some of the cost if they took their proper share in the care and the education of children which begin the moment a child is born. Of course, if this sort of mutual education were seriously undertaken women might have to go shoulder a gun, in a police army at any rate, but why not? Women in China fight in the regular army. And men might have to learn how to mix milk formulas for babies. A few have done so and retained their manhood. What men and women have to learn is that woman as a woman is not injured by doing any of the things tradition has assigned to man, nor is man as man injured by performing the duties tradition has assigned to woman.

For the old bogey of the loss of sex or sex charm through doing a particular job in the world is nothing but nonsense, repeated once more by some individual for his own self-defense for something or other. I have seen girls who never went outside their homes except to go to church or the movies or the grocery or the drugstore but who never had any more sex charm than a guinea hen, and I have seen short-haired girls in soldiers' uniforms who at the times they chose were so radiant with the famous sex appeal that men's heads turned toward them as though a strong wind were blowing upon them all from the same direction, as indeed it was. Nothing and no environment can give sex appeal to the individual, man or woman, who does not possess the technique, God-given or taught. And the teaching of it should be included as a part of that education of men and women for each other, with full training in the proper times and places to use it. Then we would be relieved of this present tedium of a spurious sex appeal injected into everything. Sex charm is a valid and important thing, and its teaching should not be left to advertisements of all sorts of things from tooth paste to the week's laundry. It is tedious to women to have to believe, as every influence tries to force them to believe, that man when he thinks of them thinks of nothing but simple sex. This belief by women removes from sex all the interest and excitement, the chance and question, the refusal or acceptance, not only of woman toward man but of man toward woman. And how tedious to the male if he believes, as he cannot be blamed for believing if he reads pages of magazines and advertisements written for women, that the minds of women are eternally fixed selfishly upon the appeal to that which he knows is only a part of his life and interest.

For the joy of sex is in variety, and I do not mean variety of individual. Nothing is more stultifying, as a matter of fact, than passing from one individual to another, pausing only long enough to discover what is common to all. No, the excitement of real sex variety is that to be found within a single relationship, based upon deep security, where between the two individuals in that relationship there is continued chance and question and freedom to refuse or to accept.

In short, sex ought to be made exciting again, and men and women should be so educated for each other that it is exciting and no longer merely a manifestation of adolescence to be kept alive as long as possible and repeated vicariously when it is dead through the tiresome and repetitive "stories of young love" to be found in too many magazines and movies. Sex is exciting only when it is a subtle and pervasive part of the relationship between men and women varying in its forms from adolescence to old age, and it dies only with death if it is properly nourished in life.

And, yet like any other part, sex loses its flavor if it loses its proper proportion to the whole of life. Antagonism between men and women is the inevitable result of the loss of this proportion between sex and the rest of their life together. Men and women must share everything in life, work at home and work abroad. Before the relationship between them can be complete and sex can take its proper proportion, they must give each other the right to do the same things if they like to do those things and can, instead of repressing each other by the old tradition that men must do one thing and women another. And so necessary is this complete relationship between men and women that without it the basic harmony of human life is lost, and discontents spring up everywhere like weeds.

What we need in our country is not merely an amendment to the constitution insisting on equality for men and women, but a new education which will really bring it about, or, to use a pedagogical term, a new orientation and technique of education, so that all education is shaped toward mutual understanding and appreciation between men and women. In such an atmosphere tradition would disappear and amendments be forgotten. And men would not have to associate women with all the unforgettable no's of childhood, and women would not have to bear the brunt of those memories, as she does now and so unjustly. And who knows if woman might not have an idea or two worth having about war and peace and the prevention of crime and the cure of poverty?

9. WOMEN AND FREEDOM

THIS education of men and women for each other might be helpful, incidentally, in the elimination of what is now known as the exceptional woman—that is, the woman who by reason of some talent and energy singles herself out or is in spite of herself singled out and, like a black swan among white, appears in those upper reaches of the arts and professions and executive offices where there are usually only men, and where her sex alone is more astonishing than anything she can possibly achieve. She is a phenomenon of the society which is peculiarly American. She does not seem singular in China, for there all sorts of women nowadays do what they please, and nobody pays any great heed to them. Only the other day some women in Chungking opened a bank—in the new and constantly bombed capital of China. If women in New York had opened a bank, what a fanfare of photography and reporting would have been the result! But these women in Chungking were not exceptional, as they would have been in New York.

In a society where woman's place was completely fixed, as it was in the old China, the exceptional woman, of course, did not appear at all. In a society completely democratic she will not appear more often than the exceptional man, because there the level of the average woman would be so high that many who now seem exceptional would not be so then. In a complete democracy where woman was free to achieve according to her ability, she would not be remarkable, as she is now merely because she is woman.

As things are today in the half-free, half-traditional state in which American women find themselves, the exceptional woman is too remarkable. She is a creature admired and despised, praised and pitied. If she deserves most of this, in Christian charity words should first be spoken for her. She is to be pitied, for it is her misfortune, so far as her personal happiness goes, that she is endowed with unusual intelligence and energy, neither of which she particularly needs for the demands of society upon her. She may even have some particular talent which, in the same measure as though she were a man, keeps her restless and dissatisfied if she is not exercising it. She cannot, however, exercise it as man would. Marriage, which she craves as naturally as he does, makes demands upon her time and thought which it does not upon him. A gifted man can develop his gift, heedless of house and child, so long as he earns enough to pay for these things. But even if a gifted woman earns, still the actual physical responsibility of house and children are hers. No one, whatever her gift, takes them from her shoulders. She does not want them lifted from her heart, but there is no freedom for her from the traditional tasks of womanhood. Man has not been educated to consider that her gift, however great, can be equal or superior to his own. He has not been educated to weigh the measure of his individual gift and hers. He keeps his freedom whether or not it is worth much to anyone. Woman, if she is so unfortunate as to have the gift, must do with it as best she can while she tends the house, the child, the man. To the callous and careless query as to why she marries and why has the home and the child at all, the answer is simply that, being a woman, she is not fulfilled unless she has the life of a woman. She is often enough as it is accused of losing her womanliness.

Sometimes the accusation is true. It cannot be denied that too many of our exceptional women are mannish, hard, ruthless, and without grace. But who can blame them? By the time woman has made her way as near to the top as she can against tradition, she has been so laughed at, so criticized, so heaped with contempt, both good-natured and ill, so soiled with the anger and envy of those less successful than she, both men and women, that she is often all that she is said to be. She could scarcely have survived otherwise unless she had been that true miracle of a woman so full of pure grace that she could have kept herself intact. But why make superhuman demands upon women that are not made upon men? The average successful man is also selfish, arrogant, and hard, and nobody blames him for it.

And yet I cannot but acknowledge that the exceptional woman, as she sometimes is, is not a likable creature, nor does she inspire other women to emulate her in any way.

She is assertive. She is ruthless in her behavior to other women and cares nothing for their well-being as a group. Her entire life and energy are absorbed in the effort to keep her place among men. These men she treats rudely if they disapprove of her, sentimentally if they approve. They admire her cautiously, hate her secretly or openly, fear her profoundly, and respect her unwillingly. She stands to them as a living argument for keeping women in the home and out of the way. Though she is more often than not both healthy and handsome, no man in his right mind would want her for his wife. It would be like marrying Cleopatra and the Statue of Liberty rolled into one, with the asp and the torch in the mixture. Though she gathers all eyes to herself when she enters an assembly, she is a solitary and restless creature, for she can no longer find joy in small ordinary events and pleasures. Her humor, if she has any, is elephantine, ponderous and pretentious, and her gaiety is ghastly because it is so determined. Her discourtesy to all women and to any man except the few whom she thinks can help her is one of the spectacles of American life at which foreigners marvel. Brilliant, beautiful, and powerful, she is a monstrosity. She is an argument for fascism—the only one I know.

Indeed, there are times, as one watches this exceptional woman, when one can understand the simple, hearty Germans. Perhaps such women as this had more than we know to do with the success of fascism. Germany had a good many exceptional women in that disconcerting gap in her history between the Kaiser and Hitler. The exceptional woman flourished in that social change. She came out of the home with a bang. If she could have come out instead with the quiet wisdom of the mature Chinese female creature she might have helped to keep liberty alive even in Germany.

For I repeat that the truly female woman cannot be made unwomanly. Whatever she is doing, she remains feminine in every look and word and act. I have seen her marching in the armies of China in an old uniform and with a gun over her shoulder. She stands at machines in Russia. I have seen her once or twice in my own country, a judge upon the bench, a doctor in an office. Wherever she is she is herself, wise, capable, unaffectedly a woman, as feminine as though she had a child at her breast or stood at the stove in her own kitchen. It does not occur to her to prove that she is as good as a man. She knows she is as good, being woman.

And yet it is true, and I have often puzzled over it, that an American woman loses her femininity more easily and quickly than do the women of other countries when she achieves some place outside the home. Why should this be except that American women, generally speaking, are undersexed? I can give no other explanation of why they are so worried about losing their essential quality as females or why they must protect so anxiously a femininity so feeble that to keep it alive they must protect it in the hothouse atmosphere of home lest it evaporate. Must women be kept continually at the grind of activities which are strictly traditionally female, lest they forget they are women?

But how can this be, I ask in wonder? For the female instinct in a strong, true woman is imbued in all her brain and body. It is not to be expressed in vague sentimental emotionalism, in chatter and frills and curled hair, in painted nails and pen-wiper hats. It is not expressed only in cooking and housekeeping and giving birth. It may not be expressed at all in these activities. Plenty of women in homes and with families are not truly feminine. No, really feminine woman cannot be and is not afraid to do or be anything she likes. *She is woman.* Whatever she does is feminine and full of woman, and she could not ape man if she tried, for she is all woman and all her thinking and breathing and being are woman, and her femaleness is herself and it cannot be taken from her or be changed, nor does she want to be changed. She wants to be what she is, a woman; and as a woman she goes anywhere and does everything, secure in her own content and being.

If women could somehow believe that they cannot cease to be women, if they are women in the first place—and if they are not deeply, truly women in the first place they are not feminine no matter what they are or wear—what a bogey would be taken from their path! It is not chastity that is the prized possession of women these days, but femininity. The two have nothing to do with each other. When a woman is cold at heart the matter of chastity is purely academic. She is incapable either of chastity or its opposite, and the number of her loves are only marks upon a tally stick.

The exceptional woman in Germany, had, of course, far more to struggle against than she has in our country. She had the unshaken determination of man to be superior to her, an opposition in its crudest and most literal form, and this determination was upheld by average women. The exceptional woman is a reproach in her freedom to those less gifted or less energetic or less conscientious women who do not wish to undertake the responsibilities of freedom. Deep in her heart, woman knows she has accepted the privileges of freedom but not the responsibilities. If one woman can achieve so much, other women ask themselves uneasily, does it show that all women ought to be more? Rather than answer that question honestly, it is easier to point fingers and cry out charges of unwomanliness and neglect of home and children and the absence of virtues which have for so long been woman's excuse. Though statistically, of course, it has already been proved that the woman who works outside the home actually gives her children more time than the so-called home woman.[1]

Pre-Nazi Germany was rather more burdened with exceptional women, however, than we are at present. There were over forty women even in the Reichstag. We have few women in the House of Representatives and one in the Senate. There were women in all German state legis-

---

[1] Shallcross, Ruth: *Should Married Women Work?* Public Affairs Pamphlet, No. 49, Public Affairs Committee, Inc., New York, 1940.

latures and city councils. Women worked in high labor organizations and co-operatives. They were judges and doctors and technicians. They made valuable contributions to national housing and schools and carried through social legislation. They resisted with all their strength the rising Nazi power. And yet the exceptional women in Germany could save neither themselves nor the average women. Together they have been forced into retreat. Today in Germany all positions outside the home, except the unimportant and the menial, are closed to women. No woman can rise to any place, however lowly, which puts her over a man. Nor can she enter universities or receive higher learning of any sort. Thus she returns to the Middle Ages.

No, the exceptional woman can save no one, not even herself, as fascism approaches, if the distance between her and the average woman is too great; and it is too great today in America as it was in Gemany. The distance is so great that the chief enemy of the exceptional woman is the average woman. And yet the exceptional woman deserves a good deal of this enmity because she allows herself to be cut off from other women by her selfishness in success, instead of using her success to lead others to better and higher places. This is folly for all, for the exceptional woman's place is insecure when it is too far above the place of other women. No woman is high enough if all women are not. And yet if one rises she should not be hated by the others—rather should she be looked upon as a hope for all. That she is hated, is only another example of the axiom that civilization is no stronger than its most barbarous member.

For there is danger in that distance between the exceptional woman and the average woman, and it is a danger for the whole people if they still have the wish to be democratic. Fascism creeps in through back doors. It is the weak, the unfulfilled, the discontented who are the back doors, and these are to be found too much among women. Anti-fascists busy themselves with commendable energy in discovering here and there in our midst a few Nazis and pro-Nazis; but they overlook the great source of danger in the masses of half-ignorant, half-idle, indolent, and discontented American women, already jealous of the exceptional women and envious too, and ready, as German women like them were ready, to pull the house down over all women if only these few could no longer be left to reproach them. These are the masses ready to run to the call of anyone clever enough to justify their futility and to sentimentalize their sex.

The German women who ran to the Nazi flag were the ignorant women who did not even know the theory of the Nazi creed. Had they read and understood it as it was expressed by Alfred Rosenberg, when he said in his *The Myth of the Twentieth Century,* "It is clear that a perpetual public influence of the women, granted in principle, would be the beginning of a notorious decadence," they might have felt alarmed. But only relatively few women were capable of reading and understanding such material. The ordinary woman avoided serious thought with its responsibilities for action. The first pro-Nazi leaders among women were those who had already taken a stand against women in government and indeed against women's social and political emancipation. They were the anti-suffragists and the anti-feminists. "None of them," says an exceptional German woman now an exile, "had ever participated in the struggle for recognition of women's rights and dignity." [2]

Who were the other German women who favored Nazism? First among them were the young women. It is alarming, in view of the retreat among the young women of our own country, to realize that there was a similar retreat in Germany and that it led them to favor Hitler, not because they knew what he would give them, but because they wanted to be sheltered and to believe in him. My heart turned cold the other day and the chill of the possible future fell across it when I heard a young American woman cry, "I'm so tired of trying to *know*—I long only to *believe!*" It was the death cry of the young German women as they ran to put themselves under the Nazi power.

There are other similarities between the pre-Hitler German women and the American women today. The masses of the German women then, like ours now, were of the lower middle class and cared nothing about politics. They thought only of themselves and their families and the small circle of their daily lives. To those lower mid-

[2] Some of the facts in this chapter are drawn from an extraordinarily interesting manuscript by Miss Toni Sender, which I hope will soon be published.

dle-class German women, therefore, it was a pleasure to have all women reduced to the common level of the *Hausfrau,* and they approved the Nazi power which could pull them down and keep them there. These women were the strongest force among women to bring in the Nazi regime. The frightening thing is that they were the home women, the good mothers.

But there were others. There was even a small group of "intelligent" women, so-called, who followed Nazism because, having tried independence, they chose retreat. They were the disappointed who had not achieved the success for which they hoped in the professions, and who had not married and were tempted by the Nazi promises to give marriage to every woman. It must remain a matter of wonder that these women, if they were really intelligent, did not question the sort of marriage that could be promised to all women. And yet it is true that in all countries there are disappointed women who would rather have any marriage than none. There will be these women as long as marriage remains the measure of woman's success as a woman. These women would in America, as in Germany, vote for Nazi men if these were the men who held out the lure of marriage to them.

But the most striking similarity between the German and the American women is in the women students. The vote taken by the women of an American college which I have cited could have come direct from Germany. It expresses exactly the attitude of those young German women students who voluntarily and consciously gave up the rights which women had won so hardly and so short a time before in Germany. True, the young German women, like the young Americans, had not themselves struggled for these rights. They accepted them as a matter of course and did not prize or even understand their value. And, like many other young women in the world today, they were discouraged by the difficulties they found before them in their longing for success. There was no sure and easy way to that success and in the face of the added obstacles of depression, always and everywhere heavier upon women than upon men, they took definite retreat into the home and the dependence upon men which Nazism offered them. They were young, let it be remembered, and the Nazis used the crassest means of emotional appeal— lights, music, mass singing and marching, and always handsome uniformed "he-men." Weak women fell before all this as before armies, victims of emotion and sex. They have remained satisfied with little positions, often without pay but always with uniforms to make them feel important and to flatter their poor vanities and to lessen the consciousness of their inferiority as human beings and their real subjection.

In all humility, as one surveys this spectacle, one must inquire whether the downfall of democracy, if it falls, will not be because we did not take sufficiently into account the weakness and folly of the masses of human beings, who know, poor, helpless souls, that they cannot achieve greatness and nobility and who, when the high demands and responsibilities of democracy are put upon them, flee from the knowledge of what they are, measured against what they are expected to be. Something like this I once saw in the eyes of a poor dull-witted fellow whom, to relieve his dire poverty, we took into our house to perform a few simple tasks. For a while he seemed happy. He was warm and he was fed, and though his mistakes were many he tried hard and no one blamed him when he failed, for we knew his limitations. But one day he came and begged to be allowed to leave. Had he another job, we inquired? No, he had no job, but he wanted to leave. Would he not soon be hungry and cold and homeless again? Yes, he admitted, he would. We pressed him a little. Had we not been kind enough to him? A strange look came into his dull eyes. Oh, yes, we had been very kind, it was not that. Then what? we asked. The strange look struggled to express itself, "Ma'am, it's this—you're such thinkin' kind of people." It was the discomfort of the incompetent in the presence of the competent, the unease of those who cannot think in the presence of those who think because they cannot help it. We understood and let him go, but we have never forgotten him. There are millions like him whom democracy cannot comfort because it does not take cognizance of their real being.

To take cognizance of the real being—this is all that is necessary for happiness. If men and women could really know each other, not only as the individuals they marry or as relatives and hirelings, but as human beings at work together on a job, that job being the managing of human society, they could take cognizance each of the other's being. That is, each would demand of the other only what ought to be demanded, not more and certainly not less. As it is, they do demand too much of each other and at the same time too little. And their demands are based upon and shaped by tradition rather than upon that which each really should want of the other—a spontaneous and free co-operation which will give all individuals, men and women, the greatest freedom consistent with equal opportunity in life and work.

When I look at these words which I have just set down I perceive that unaware I have arrived at a goal. I have not searched for that goal. I have wandered along the paths of freedom for men and women, of freedom from the burdens they have put upon each other, on the whole unwittingly. I have pursued the possibilities of happiness for both, whether these have been tried or not. All the ways and paths which have covered the earth in their direction from east to west lead me, I find, to this: that happiness for men and women is in the greatest freedom for both that is consistent with equal opportunity. Freedom without opportunity is meaningless.

Free men and free women, working on equal terms together in all the processes of life—and what is this but democracy? For in our preoccupation with nations and peoples and races, let us remember again that there is a division still more basic than these in human society. It is the division of humanity into men and women. Men and women against each other destroy all other unity in life. But when they are for each other, when they work together, the fundamental harmony exists, the foundation upon which may be built all that they desire.

EPILOGUE
WOMEN AND "LIBERATION"

THIRTY years have passed since I wrote this little book, *Of Men and Women*. Thirty years! It is the lifetime of a generation in China, the land where I was a child and grew to womanhood and maturity. That China is no more. Land and people—yes, of course they are still there, but how changed! Communism rules, and Communism has totally altered the relationship between Chinese men and women. For practical reasons Communism compels women to come out of the home and contribute their share to national labor and industrialization. The theory is that no nation can solve its industrial problems with half its human resources in brains and hands. The family system is considered too expensive. One woman can do more and must do more than care for her own family. Hence for the first time in centuries the family unit in China was broken up by Communism and dispersed. Children were put into children's homes or day care centers. Old people, heretofore cherished by their families, were put into homes for the aged. The state became the first consideration.

There was of course a political reason for this Communist attack upon the traditional Chinese family system. The family system there was the social stronghold, units consisting possibly of hundreds of individuals, to whom the safety and welfare of the family came first, ahead of patriotism, nationalism, and finally of Communism. It was essential, from the Communist point of view, that the family be broken apart, the children taken away as early as three years of age, the young adults put to work, and the old men and women, with their traditions and memories, segregated. How successful this fragmentation has been we do not know, since

Americans have no direct access to mainland China. Rumor, however, points to the possibility that it has not been wholly successful and I am inclined to believe this to be true. Nevertheless, the experience that Chinese women have had under Communist direction will probably have changed them. Certainly the young women, who have known nothing except Communism, will not be like their mothers and grandmothers. Today they are not only working in modern industries, they are also serving in the armed forces, and since they were always strong and from birth and by tradition never pampered, it is the less likely that they will ever give up their independence.

Yet, human nature being what it is, some sort of family life undoubtedly still goes on. I saw pictures by a French newspaperman taken recently in the city of Nanking, in the province of Kiangsu, China, a city where I lived for many years. It is a mighty city, the Southern Capital of China, famous through six thousand years of history. There are new high-rise buildings there now, but men still haul loaded carts as they used to do in the days when that city was my home. I wonder if the great city wall is there. I have not heard that it is gone. But I read in the article with the pictures that a great bridge has been built across the wide Yangtze river between Nanking and Pengpu, the river port opposite. Until recently, when this bridge was completed, great ferries carried people, freight, vehicles, even trains, across the river. Now the bridge is there and in constant use. It is not likely that the Chinese will ever go back to the old ferries. I use the bridge as a symbol. The Chinese will remain Chinese. Their life will continue as it has for thousands of years. But they will live in new ways and with new tools. Practicality will be the keyword rather than tradition.

Here in my own country what have been the changes that have taken place between men and women in the last thirty years? How would I change now this little book I wrote so long ago, and so soon after I myself had changed countries and cultures? As I read its pages again, I am surprised how little there would be to change. True, the "gunpowder women" I wrote of thirty years ago are beginning to explode, as I foretold. Let me underscore *beginning*, for the women's liberation movement has only begun the explosion. It may be only a flash—time will tell. Nevertheless, it is, I feel, a preliminary warning of much to come. To change the symbol, let me say there is a ground swell among women all over the world which will break into white-capped waves in one country and another. Two Prime Ministers, one in vast India, one in little Israel, are both eminently successful women. Human and humane, politically astute and fearless, they prove that women can achieve notable ends, yet without the traits of masculinity. Here in my own country, I sense, rather than know, a profound though not publicly expressed acceptance of the possibility of a woman as President. True, this will not be a fact in the near future, unless the right woman appears—and she might appear at any moment. I say future, not necessarily far future. Thirty years ago this was not true.

I attribute this possibility to two changes that have taken place: one in woman and one in man. The change in woman is that women are less jealous of each other, more loyal to each other, and less inclined to believe in the leadership of men simply because they are men. I do not say for one moment that they value men less or like them less or consider them less necessary to life and happiness. On the contrary, indeed! I feel today's women realize as never before the necessity of men's love and companionship and they admire generously the achievements of men. But they are more selective about men. Women today tend, I think, to judge a man first as a human being, and only secondly as a man. Thirty years ago I think the reverse was true. This change is true, moreover, in women's attitude toward women. Women are increasingly judging women first as human beings and only secondly as women —or to put it more precisely, as females.

This change, seemingly simple, is in fact profound. If women and men judge each other first as human beings and only secondly as sex objects, then we are setting the atmosphere for true equality between the sexes. The change, of course, is the result of what has happened during the last thirty years—namely, a continuing war. The Second World War, the Korean War, the war in Southeast Asia, have forced women to become more and more self-sufficient, not only emotionally and psychologically, but in practical ways. Most women of this generation have had, for some period at least, to be both father and mother to their children. Many have had to go to work in offices and factories in order to eke out their incomes. They have learned to know themselves and their own powers. They have learned to recognize the good qualities of other women, and as a result of mutual admiration have lost much of their former pettiness. There is a camaraderie among women nowadays which is heartening and enlarging to all. True, women are still not in the highest echelons of administration, but the atmosphere is getting ready for progress there, too. If women can regard other women as human beings first and if they do not accord to an unworthy man, merely because he is a man, a position he does not deserve, that is progress toward a better future. I was pleased the other day to hear a certain daughter of mine, the young mother of three sons and two daughters, varying in ages from seven to thirteen, programming the week's household work equally between boys and girls. Boys took their turns at dishwashing and girls their turns at bringing in wood for the fireplaces, for example. When I commented favorably on their mutual responsibilities, she remarked practically:

"Men and women have to learn how to do everything nowadays. The old separations are gone."

Let me hasten to say next that men have changed, too. They expect more of women, they demand more of women. Male eyes follow a pretty girl as unfailingly as ever, but they are eyes that carry more than a sexual question. There is plenty of simple physical sex, of course—and physical sex is, by the way, essentially a very simple business in spite of all the books written on the subject— but there is in the male calculation a question and a demand for something more, if a relationship is to continue. Brains are surprisingly often appreciated. Men enjoy being amused, diverted, stimulated to thought and consideration of new ideas, and once having had this new and surprising experience with a woman, they learn to demand it. This has, of course, an important effect on women, leading them to further self-development.

It remains to be seen what changes will take place in both men and women when we no longer have wars that separate them. We have had wars before, of course, but we have never before had long wars in Asia, and our men have never before had years with Asian women. Asian women are born wise and old in ways which western women know nothing about. Asia never had an age of Knighthood's Flower and all that, Asian women were never pampered and made much of by men or by anyone else. When a girl child was born she soon learned to fend for herself and get what she wanted in any way she could, by force, cunning, or charm. The thousands of half-American children in Asia today, stateless because Asians consider the child the possession and responsibility of the father, attest to the successful tactics of the Asian women. But sex and money aside, what effect will the years in old Asia have on our American men? No one knows. On fact is clear: it is well that American women have had the experience of having to think for themselves and do for themselves, in this long interval when so many thousands of our men have been away.

This new independence is already showing itself in several ways. The most notable is the new sexual freedom. It is still customary, although no longer necessary, for a man and woman who are going to live together to get married, for each is more secure with the ceremony—or are they? I have been shaken since I recently argued the case with a young woman, a very young woman, whose marriage, two years before, had broken up. She had, she said, been very happy the first year. Her husband was a senior in college and she had gone to work herself in order to pay the expenses of his last year. Then, one day when she was emptying the pockets of a suit before sending it to the cleaners, she had found a letter and a love poem from another girl. Confronted when he came home, he confessed that there was another girl. The wife then discovered that she herself was pregnant, and the marriage was patched up, the baby born in due course, a beautiful boy, and all this time the other girl clung to the husband, though promising not to do so. The upshot of it was separation—a divorce was too expensive—and after a period of indecision, the young husband confused and the young wife hurt and angry, the marriage apparently hopeless, the wife began to live with another young man, a kinder man, with a successful business of his own.

"But a divorce—" I suggested.

She shook her head. "I'm free anyway," she said.

"But does this man want to marry you someday?" I inquired.

"I've never asked, he's never said," was the reply. "Besides, what's the use of another scrap of paper? We'll live together as long as we're happy. I'm too depressed to live alone."

"But the baby—"

"He'll always have me."

"No family?"

"Families are out," she said flatly.

Later, talking over the situation with another young woman, herself happily married thus far, I was surprised and saddened, though not shocked, to have her agree with the young mother.

"Things aren't the way they used to be," she said.

She summed it with a cliché, but she had summed it. The long-haired young men, the pants-suited girls, the immediacy of sex intercourse, its casualness, its lack of any connections with what used to be called love, the music, so strange with the wailing voices, one voice like another, the eternal strumming of guitars, lonely dancing, each individual apart from the other, man separate from woman—yes, it is true. Things are different. It is the music that conveys the difference to me more clearly than anything else—the return to the folk music, the primitive, the individual complaint, music revealing loneliness and confusion. It is historically true that in times of national disorder, there is in any people a tendency to revert to individualistic folk music. It is an instinctive music, an expression of profound dissent and discontent. Music is, of course, the revelation not only of individual fear, pessimism, and threat, but when it becomes as universal in its form and content as are today's songs, beat and thrumming in the United States, not to mention other parts of the world where it is also appearing, then it must be observed as the revealing of revolutionary threat. It is to be taken seriously.

I am reminded by all this of a previous era in my life—the

revolutionary era in my Chinese life, which ended in the victory of Communism there. For I was born into that era. It was near the end of a dynasty, always a dangerous period through the centuries of China's many dynasties. There were, of course, safeguards for maintaining order until a new emperor appeared from among the people. The process was democratic. Upon the decline of a dynasty, ending in the death of the last emperor, with no heir apparent left, young men of all classes throughout the empire gathered personal armies and fought each other until one young man emerged as the victor over all the others.

During this process, which might be short or long, the people remained undisturbed and the functions of the government went on. Two strong forces made this possible; first, a highly selective and intelligent civil service, and second, the firmly established traditional and powerful family system. For centuries these two forces remained inviolable. The change came as a result of the impact of the West through colonialism and its arsenals of explosive weapons—such weapons as China had invented centuries before and rejected as inhumane and uncivilized. Her mistake, of course, was in not realizing the generation gap between nations, a gap as valid as that between individuals. At any rate, without going into lengthy description at this moment, let me say that the civil service fell into decay as a result of the stopping of the Imperial Examinations, and the traditional family system broke under the impact of the acquaintance of young Chinese with the Western peoples. Young Chinese were allowed to go abroad for education and they came back with new ideas.

In fact, there is nothing new to me in the behavior of young people here in my own country at the present moment. I have been through it all before, but in China and in my own youth. The flouting of parents and elders, the uprisings and violence of students, the demand for freedom from traditional marriage and the demand for liberty in sex experiment—it is all old stuff to me. I have seen it before in its manifold forms in daily life, in revolutionary music, in revolutionary literature—I have seen it all and long ago. In China it ended in the overthrow of the government,

centuries old, and then a vacuum of ten years of no central government—and finally Communism. It is easy to overthrow a government but very difficult to build a new one, as the young Chinese
found. The result of their failure was that when Communism came
in it found its work already half done. The civil service and the
traditional family system, China's two establishments, were gone.
All the Communists had to do, once the world war was ended, was
to set up their own political system and destroy the last vestiges of
the family system.

I recount in brief this long and dramatic story, which I observed
through experience, because I observe and experience here and
now the same events, the same trends, that took place in China. I
consider the breakdown of the family as most serious. When marriage is no longer considered necessary between men and women,
when children are born without families to be responsible for them,
then the end result is that the state must take over. Communism
took over Chinese children, placed them in institutions, fed, clothed
and indoctrinated them. They looked to the state as their protector
and benefactor. The head of that state was and is their father
figure. This happened in China, the oldest and greatest of civilized
nations. It can certainly happen here in The United States, the
youngest of the great nations, the least established in its traditions.

I am not given to prophecies and warnings. I simply say, however,
that what has happened elsewhere can happen here, if men and
women in their new freedom with each other allow it to happen.
The family system here, too, is beginning to weaken. Women demand equality with men not only economically, legally and socially,
but also sexually. Before such demands are met, and they should
be and will be met and this without doubt, let men and women, in
equal responsibility, take thought of the child. A man and woman
may not be a family, but with the birth of a child, wanted or not,
the two become three and three is a family. A family, in my opinion
and experience, must be a responsible unit—responsible for providing a stable environment for the child, who is the next generation,
the human continuum.

In short, and in conclusion, men and women, in all freedom,

may be free only insofar as their freedom does not destroy the nation. There must be basic foundations for the security of the nation. Neither man nor woman is wholly free. Whether the individual wishes, declares, demands total freedom, it is impossible, for such freedom does not exist save in drug-induced dreams. The smallest pebble cast into a pool creates ripples which cannot, by the law of action and reaction, be stopped.

What more can be said? Women are now liberated. So are men. What will be the result of such liberation? I look about me and see all that I saw thirty years ago in China—angry students, rebellious young, frenetic music, wild experiment, rebellion—rebellion—rebellion. Did a young woman say to me the other day "the family is finished"? Yes, I heard that too, thirty years ago.

And Communism came marching in.